Short Stories
for
Long Rainy Days

Short Stories for Long Rainy Days

SIMPLE TALES OF LIFE AND LOVE

KATHERINE ANNE DOUGLAS

PROMISE PRESS

An Imprint of Barbour Publishing

Acknowledgements

The author thanks Debbie Peterson for her editorial review and suggestions. A special thank you to Susan Johnson at Barbour Publishing, Inc. for her part in making this author's dream a reality.

Published by Promise Press, an imprint of Barbour Publishing, Inc., P.O. Box 719, Uhrichsville, Ohio 44683, http://www.barbourbooks.com

 Member of the
Evangelical Christian
Publishers Association

Printed in the United States of America.

Dedication

This book is dedicated with
love and appreciation to my dear parents,
Kenny and Betty Vicary.

Contents

Preface

If you enjoy an occasional break from life's daily demands, but are short on time, this collection of short stories is for you. The stories and characters are fictional. My hope, however, is that you will take to heart the things within this collection that are not of fiction: the power of the gospel of Jesus Christ to change lives and the power of love to change attitudes. So, grab a cup of hot chocolate, kick off your shoes, let the rain outside provide a restful background cadence, and settle in for a few minutes of light reading.

Enjoy!
Katherine Anne Douglas

CHAPTER 1

Premeditated

Lily Blackstone's right arm shot out from under her bedding to silence the alarm clock. Her morning dream had been shattered. She kept her face buried deeply in her pillow, her hand still clutching the clock. This was vacation. Why had she set her alarm for five o'clock in the morning? Her hair. She had an appointment to get her hair cut. She released her grip on the alarm clock and slowly sat up, mentally appraising the day she had planned.

Lily was methodical and organized in her approach to life. Since her high school days she had always kept a daily schedule, both in her head and in a pocket-sized daily planner she carried in her purse. She could not tolerate clutter or disorder in her life or her surroundings. Her apartment was spotless; her appearance impeccably neat. Routine and punctuality were the hallmarks of her life. She did not begrudge others their spontaneity or disorganization. In some ways such things intrigued her, but only fleetingly. A person did not have to live in disarray or confusion. Life might bring both and often did, but people could bring order and organization if they simply had a mind to do so. And Lily Blackstone did. Life and other people threatened to throw her into turmoil on a regular basis, but she maintained her decorum. She was never detoured for long from her ordered course. Lily's smiles were not rare, but she seldom laughed. She was not particularly happy, but she was quietly content with her orderly life.

She rose and quickly made her bed. She showered and slipped into some shorts and a loose-fitting tank top. She meticulously applied her makeup and arranged her naturally curly brown hair into a French braid. Pulling her hair back gave an almost austere look to her face. Her blue-gray eyes assessed the reflection in the mirror and from the braid she pulled a solitary curl out to hang loosely on each side of her face. She had always thought her lips were too wide for her face and, therefore, wore a light shade of lipstick. Her teeth were straight and white, thanks to four years of braces and brushing her teeth faithfully after every meal.

Lily had decided she would have her nails done today as well. Vacation never meant a deviation from the pristine appearance she was consistently careful to maintain. She did not do it out of vanity; it was simply part of the ordered precision of her life. Satisfied with her appearance, she went to her kitchen for her morning cup of hot cocoa and single piece of toast.

She sat at her desk and continued her study of the Book of Romans for the next hour. Her exhaustive Bible concordance and other study guides were placed back into their respective places at the end of her study time and then she retrieved her prayer journal. Like her daily calendar, Lily had kept a prayer journal from the day she had become a Christian. She had gone through many notebooks in the ten years since then, but she had saved them all and meticulously carried over prayers that had yet to be answered from year to year and book to book. Her prayers were as orderly as every other area of her life, but they were genuine and sincere. As she had done every day for the last ten of her twenty-four years, Lily closed her two hours of study and prayer with praises to the God she loved deeply. She was glad that God was a God of order.

In an adjacent apartment, Scott Ferguson rolled over to look at the time. He had meant to get up before nine o'clock, but he just couldn't pull himself out of bed. He stretched his lanky, six-foot-six-inch frame the length of his bed and again wondered why the American mattress industry couldn't make a standard-sized bed that fit the standard-sized American male. He picked up the spongy orange ball on the floor by his bed and arched it easily into the small hoop across the room. He ran his hand through his thinning blond hair and plodded out to the kitchen to see if he had anything to eat for breakfast. He poured himself a cup of coffee, thinking his coffeemaker with the delayed timer was the best gift his mother had ever gotten him. He used to keep it in his bedroom so he wouldn't even have to get out of bed before having his first cup in the morning. But he found he was constantly running later than usual after a month or so of that practice! The aroma often helped entice him out of bed in the morning, so he had decided it was better to keep the coffeemaker in the kitchen like most people did. Today, however, he had ignored the aroma for some time before getting up. He grabbed a handful of cookies from a bag he'd left on the counter the previous night and went to the window. The apartment complex was still, as it usually was, and the smell that drifted up to his nostrils was a peculiar blend of cut grass and engine exhaust. He waved at his neighbor who was pulling out of his parking place, his rusted, old truck the violator of the morning quiet and the perpetrator of the exhaust fumes.

"Hey, Scott! How are ya?" his neighbor said, returning his greeting and stopping just below Scott's window.

"Fine. I'm on vacation the next couple of weeks. Wanna shoot some baskets tonight?"

"Maybe when I get home from work. I'll give you a buzz." Scott held up his cup of coffee in agreement and watched Hank drive away. Scott breathed a quick prayer for Hank. He had been talking to Hank for a long time about Jesus Christ, but all his talk had fallen on deaf ears. Scott was encouraged that Hank would still socialize with him; obviously, he hadn't put him off completely. There were a few people in their complex who avoided him—he laughed at his own joke—religiously.

"I praise you, Father, that You are a God who hears the quick, spontaneous prayers of Your children! You are God of the spontaneous and the impulsive! YES!" he said, instinctively raising his cup of coffee and spilling some of the hot liquid on his hand in the process. "Yowch!" He quickly transferred the cup to his other hand and wiped the wet one on his gym shorts. A boy came walking across the parking lot below him and looked up at Scott with a grin, his eyes squinting in the morning sunshine.

"Hey, Jason!" Scott called down. "Visiting your mom today?"

The young boy with his distinctive cowlick nodded. "Hi, Scotty! Wanna shoot some hoops?"

"See if you can round up some kids around the block and I'll be out in a few minutes."

Jason's face brightened. "Yeah! We'll yell for ya. I'll go get Dan and Mick and some of the other guys!" He was off and around the end of the building before Scott could say anything else. A knock sounded at his door and Scott swallowed the last of his bitter coffee.

"Is that the woman of my dreams? The love of my life? Is she up at the crack of dawn for me?" He opened the door to face Lily. He pulled her into his embrace, but his kiss landed awkwardly on her ear instead of her lips as Lily turned her head and held her hands up against his bare chest.

"Scott Ferguson! You're not even dressed yet! Do you always answer the door in your pajamas?" Lily brushed past him, going to an end table to pick up his leftover bowl of popcorn and empty can of soda pop from the night before. "And it's hardly the crack of dawn," she said over her shoulder.

"Don't tell me," Scott said, following her to his kitchen. "You got up at six A.M. just to get your last vacation as a single woman off to its earliest possible start." He set down his coffee cup and reached once more for Lily. "No good-morning kiss?"

Lily lifted her face and stood on tiptoe to give Scott a kiss on the cheek, ignoring his exaggerated puckered lips. "That was certainly a no good-morning kiss," he said, talking through his puckered, unkissed lips.

"Well, you smell like a mixture of sleep, coffee, and last night's Chinese food. Do me a favor—don't ever order garlic chicken once we're married." She wet the dishcloth and wiped the counter up in one deft motion. "And no, I got up at five. . . ."

"Five! Five as in five in the morning?" The cookie Scott was about to put in his mouth stopped in midair.

"I've got a lot to do today," Lily said calmly. "My hair appointment, for one thing, and a trip to make a final decision on my wedding dress. I'm still debating between two patterns. Aunt Martha can do either one; I just haven't decided which I like better."

"Five in the morning?" Scott hadn't heard much beyond that. He went to his couch and plopped down with a groan. "I'm marrying an alien," he mumbled. "She gets up at five in the morning on the first day of her vacation." He laid his arm across his eyes.

Lily kept wiping the kitchen counter and table while she talked. "I had to have my study and prayer time first. Did you have yours yet?"

"I do my best prayin' and studying at night, sweet Lily. You know I'm not a morning person."

"Hey, Scotty! Ya ready?"

Scott jumped up at the sound of Jason's call and went to the window. "I'll be right out, Jason. Hi, guys!" he waved at the other boys with Jason. They acknowledged his greeting with a combination of grunts and briefly raised heads in greeting.

"You're going out to play basketball already? I thought

you were going to get your car worked on today," Lily interjected from the kitchen.

"There's no rush. I've got two weeks off, remember? And I've got you to run me around if I need it." Scott went to put on his shorts and a tee shirt.

"Scott!" Lily called in exasperation. "We've got a lot to do for the wedding!"

"We've got six months yet, Lil," he called back from behind his bedroom door.

"Four months, Scott. Four months. It's June and October is coming quickly."

"We've got plenty of time." He went into the bathroom and closed the door.

"Scott, big weddings take a lot of planning. Things don't just fall into place overnight." *How many times have we had this conversation?* Lily wondered. She looked at her watch. "Listen, I've got to go. . . ."

"Your hair's fine the way it is, Lily," Scott peeked his head around the door, toothpaste running down his chin while he waved his toothbrush at her for emphasis. "This is what I look like every morning, princess. Still want to marry me?"

She shook her head with a smile. "You're impossible."

"So my mother tells me." He came out of the bathroom wiping the remains of toothpaste off his face. "A good-morning kiss now? Just for practice?" Lily returned his gentle kiss. "Better?" he asked.

She rolled her eyes and shook her head. "Don't do the garlic anymore. I'll come back after my first few stops in case you get your car in and need a ride home." She picked up her purse and headed out the door.

Scott went over to the window again. "I'm coming, guys! Hey! Ask that good-lookin' woman if she'll join us!" The boys snickered and poked one another in the ribs as Lily exited the building and waved back at Scott with a small smile and a shake of her head.

Scott put on his socks and shoes and grabbed his ball. He hit the pavement dribbling, throwing his young companions into an immediate, laugh-filled frenzy for the basketball. The early morning's quiet came to an abrupt end.

At her first stop, Lily had gotten her hair trimmed. Her stylist had pulled it up and back, letting ringlets hang softly around her neck and face. Lily planned to try on some wedding veils and headpieces and wanted her hair up like it would be for the wedding. As the morning progressed, she checked off the stops she had on her list: hairdresser's, post office, pharmacy, and the fabric store.

She finally made her decision on the dress pattern, the simpler of the two styles with long sleeves that buttoned at the wrists. The neckline was simple and modest and would not detract from the sapphire and pearl necklace that had been her great-great-grandmother's. The pendant was a large, pale blue sapphire set in gold and miniature pearls. It hung from two strands of pearls. Some people might think it gaudy; Lily thought it the most exquisite, elegant piece of jewelry she had ever seen. It had been in her mother's family for five generations; every firstborn daughter from the original Lily Rose Langston had inherited it on her wedding day. It was the traditional "something blue." Someday Lily and Scott would have a daughter, and she too would wear it. Lily touched her hand to throat and smiled to herself. Continuity and tradition were such wonderful things. They gave a person. . .permanence. Solidity.

She pictured in her mind the rest of her dress. The ivory satin would have a fitted bodice and then gently flare from the waist. Like the necklace, pearl buttons would be at the sleeves and down the back of the dress to the waistline. There she would have her aunt fashion a delicate cluster of fine blue satin ribbon that would hang in streamers down the back of her gown. It would be perfect. Her bridesmaids would wear gowns in the same shade of pale blue. Scott would look so handsome in his black tuxedo. It would be the perfect wedding, she just knew it.

She pulled into the bridal shop to inspect the selection of headpieces. She knew she was late in ordering a headpiece, but nothing seemed quite right. By the time she left the bridal shop, she had made her decision. She would wear some of the satin ribbon wound in her hair. It would be in keeping with the simple elegance of her gown.

When Lily returned to the apartment, she was relieved to see Scott was not still playing basketball. She wanted him with her to finalize arrangements with the caterer. She took her packages to her apartment and promptly put everything away. She checked her list again, methodically marking off what had been done, and noting what else needed to be done today, tomorrow, and the next day, cross-checking her list with her calendar. She walked back over to Scott's apartment and knocked on the door.

"Come in, my precious Lily!" she heard him yell in what she called his "jungle warble."

"Scott, you really should keep your door locked," she said as she entered. She looked at him in dismay. "You haven't even showered yet!"

"What's the rush? I'm on vacation! I thought we could take a dip in the pool. Want something to drink?"

Lily followed him into the kitchen. "When are you going to take your car in? And we have an appointment to see the caterer!" She was trying, unsuccessfully, to hold her irritation in check.

"I'll take the car in tomorrow. Don't we have time for a swim?"

"Scott. I just got my hair done. Remember?" She gathered up an assortment of magazines and stacked them neatly in the magazine rack she had bought him the previous Christmas.

"Oh, yeah. It looks nice, princess, but I like it down. You're going to wear it down for the wedding, aren't you?" He grabbed one of the magazines she had just put away. "Hey, look at this." He scanned the table of contents and began turning the pages, her newly styled hair almost forgotten.

"No, I'm planning to wear it like this."

"You never wear it down and just hanging loosely—like it was when we met. Whatta ya think of this?" He thrust the magazine at her.

" 'Hanging loosely' is not vogue right now, Scott. Think

of what?" She puzzled over the picture of horses he held in front of her.

"Going to one of those dude ranches out west for our honeymoon. It would be different! A wild time! Something new to try!"

"Try riding a horse for the first time in my life on our honeymoon? Scott, be serious!"

"I am. What's unique or original about going to Maine?" he asked.

"It will be new for us! I've already gotten our route planned and the places we'll stay and—"

"My dear Lily Rose, I appreciate your planning, but how about a little adventure? A little spontaneity? A 'walk on the wild side'?" He spun around and pulled her to him to dance.

"You know I don't do 'spontaneity' well. Listen," she said, changing the subject and wiggling out of his embrace at the same time. "Why don't you take a shower? I'll take your car over and leave it there so Ray can start working on it today or tomorrow. You can pick me up in my car and we'll get to the caterer's on time."

"No swim, huh?"

"Scott Michael!"

"Okay! Okay!" He held his hands up in mock surrender as he started towards the bathroom. "I think my keys are on my dresser. If not, look in my jeans' pocket," he said, closing the door behind him.

"How can a person live like this?" Lily mumbled as she quickly made Scott's bed and gathered up scattered clothes and other paraphernalia. She finally found his keys in his tennis shoe and left for the auto repair shop.

An hour later, Lily was still at the repair shop and it was past time for their meeting with the caterer. She tried telephoning Scott with no success. Another half hour later, he pulled into the shop. He reached over to open the door for her. Lily was livid.

"Sorry, honey. Jason and his mom needed a ride to the store and it took longer than she thought it would. We can make it to the caterer's—"

"No, we can't. The appointment was for forty minutes ago." Lily was used to Scott's unpredictable—and unreliable —time management, but sometimes it wore on her patience. Today it wore on her patience. "Please, Scott. Try helping me a little more with the wedding plans, would you?" she asked.

"I'll try harder, Lily Rose. That reminds me, " he said, snapping his fingers. "My brother won't be able to make the wedding."

Lily was dumbstruck. "He what?" she asked, her mouth hanging open in disbelief. Scott reached over from the steering wheel and put his finger under her chin, closing her mouth for her.

"You're not a fish, my flower. He can't make it—decided he can't afford the airfare. I'll ask Alan to be best man."

"Then who will be the other groomsman?"

"Why do we need another one? We'll just have two!" he said, turning into the parking lot of their apartment complex.

"Because we have three bridesmaids, Scott, and the girls already have ordered their dresses."

"Oh." He sat thinking for a few seconds. "Well, I'll have to think of someone else. Maybe Blake or Murray. . ." The two of them got out of Lily's car and walked to their building.

"Let's do something exciting this week, Lily," Scott said, changing the subject and interrupting Lily's train of thought. She retrieved her keys from her purse as they arrived at her door.

"Like what?" she said absently. Scott followed her into her apartment and promptly went to the refrigerator for something to drink.

"Oh, I don't know. Try scuba diving or take a ride in a hot air balloon or get married. . . ." He gave her a smile with uplifted eyebrows.

"We are getting married. In October. And we have plenty else to do this week without scuba diving." She looked up at him with a smile. "I would like to take a ride in a hot air balloon. It sounds both exciting and romantic. . . ." Her dreamy look ended in a shrug of her shoulders. "But probably too expensive."

"What's money for but to spend?"

"We're spending it on a big wedding." Lily began cutting up an apple. She halved it, cored it, and then cut it into neat segments, handing one to Scott.

"I hate big weddings, Lily. I hate wearing a tie and rented shoes that have harbored who knows how many pairs of smelly feet!" He popped the whole apple wedge into his mouth.

"I know, Scott, but it's important to my mother and to me." She chewed reflectively on the small piece of apple she had bitten off one of the remaining segments. "By the way, what do you think of Tom?"

"That guy she's been dating? Seems like an okay guy to me." Scott began pulling items out of the refrigerator and cupboard. "I think it's neat she's found someone after being alone for so many years. Your dad died when you were in junior high, right? That's a lot of years to fly solo."

He spread some peanut butter on a piece of bread and then placed slices of banana on it. Lily watched him spread some mayonnaise on the other slice of bread and then put the sandwich together.

"Thank You, Lord, for peanut butter, banana, and mayo sandwiches," he said before taking his first bite. He exaggerated a groan of pleasure and brought his sandwich and soda pop with him as he sat down beside Lily on the sofa. He pushed the sandwich in front of her face.

"Come on, princess. You've got to try this. It's the world's best sandwich," he said, still chewing.

"It gets more disgusting to me every time you make one," Lily said with a grimace, pushing the sandwich away.

"Don't know what you're missing," Scott said, taking another large bite.

Lily rose to get another apple segment and put away everything Scott had left on her counter.

"I'll get that when I'm done, Lily," he mumbled around the food in his mouth, simultaneously waving the sandwich at her. Lily seemed not to hear him.

"She really does seem taken with him. She's never dated anyone since Dad died. How long has she known Tom? Two weeks? Three?" she asked. She put things away and wiped off the counter, coming back to sit next to her fiancé.

"I dunno. Good for her. I like Tom." He took a sip of his beverage and once more offered a bite of his sandwich to Lily. She turned up her nose and finished the last of her apple as the telephone rang. Scott finished his sandwich and listened to one side of the brief conversation.

"I suppose we could. . . . Do you want me to bring anything?" Lily hesitated and then replied before saying goodbye. "That was my mother," she said to Scott. "She wants us to come over for supper tonight."

"Great! I could use one of your mom's delicious meals." Scott disposed of his soda pop can and returned to the couch. He handed another apple segment to Lily before lying down and resting his head on her lap.

"Mom sounded. . .strange. . ." Lily said almost to herself.

Scott closed his eyes contentedly. "Strange? Strange how?"

"I don't know. She was. . .giggly. She said she didn't know what we'd have to eat—that she'd think of something."

"Your mother said that?" Scott opened one eye. "The ultimate organizer? The one who steeped her only daughter in ritual, tradition, organization, and arranging the clothes in her closet by color and function?"

"We're not that bad," Lily responded, absently running her fingers through Scott's hair just above his right ear.

Right, he thought, but didn't say so. "Giggly? Since when is Iris Blackstone giggly?" he asked. "I'll bet your mother has never giggled in her life."

"I know. Well, let me call the caterer and set up another appointment," Lily got up suddenly and Scott's head fell back onto the sofa. "I'll try to make the appointment for first thing in the morning. We'll check on your car after we get done there."

"How early is 'first thing in the morning'?" Scott asked, keeping his eyes closed against the late afternoon sun coming in the window.

"As soon as someone is there we can talk to. Hopefully before nine o'clock," she answered. Scott groaned, but Lily did not hear him.

It was well past 6:30 by the time Scott and Lily arrived at Iris Blackstone's house. Scott had played some basketball with Hank and had to shower again. Lily had called her mother to tell her they would be late and her mother had simply laughed.

"No problem," she said. "I haven't started it yet anyway. I was. . .busy," she had said, giggling again.

"Maybe she's having a nervous breakdown," Lily whispered to Scott as they walked up to the house.

"Your mother wouldn't permit herself the luxury of a nervous breakdown any more than you would, pet," said Scott. "She doesn't have time for it. Too many other projects." They walked into the house, Lily calling out a greeting.

"Hi, kids!" Tom greeted them affably, holding out his hand to shake hands with Scott. "Iris is in the backyard. We decided to grill something."

Scott and Lily followed Tom through the house, carefully stepping around a can of paint, a tray, and a host of rollers. "Watch your step," Tom cautioned. "We've been busy painting all day. Want to spruce up the old place before selling it."

"Selling it? Mom is selling the house?" Lily looked to her mom as they came outside once again.

Her mother, short and slightly overweight, beamed a smile at them and lifted her face to give Scott a kiss and her daughter a hug. To Lily's astonishment, she then turned to Tom, and kissed him too with a murmured "I missed you, darling."

Lily looked agape at Scott, who flashed her a surprised grin and shrugged his shoulders. Iris seemed to notice none of this and Tom, Lily thought, looked curiously smug.

"Yes," Iris replied, turning back to the grill, "I am selling the house. I'm ready for a change. We're just getting it spruced up a bit before putting it on the market." She gave the skewered meat and vegetables a turn on the grill.

"So Tom told us. Where are you planning to buy?" asked Lily, somewhat dumbfounded by her mother's news.

"We'll tell you that in a few minutes," her mother said, smiling at Tom.

" 'We—'," began Lily, but her mother brushed her questioning look aside.

"It's almost ready!" Iris announced. While Scott went to help Tom with the beverages, Lily and her mother quickly finished setting the table. Their discussion revolved around Lily's wedding attire.

Once they had sat down for their meal, Tom offered thanks for the food. He passed the platter of shish kebabs to Lily, who continued her conversation with her mother regarding the wedding. Tom and Scott discussed the current baseball standings and then talked about the four of them going to the next Detroit Tigers' home game. The mealtime was amicable and pleasant. Tom insisted on helping Iris clear the table and kept telling Lily to "stay where you are" while he gathered up dishes and brought out coffee or more lemonade for each of them. Lily kept watching glances and looks pass between her mother and Tom. She thought they might have been holding hands under the table during the meal.

Is my mother in love with Tom? she wondered. She certainly didn't seem to be herself, and Tom was almost disgusting in his undisguised, frequent, beaming smiles at Iris. When Lily accidentally dropped her napkin on the ground, she bent down to pick it up. Looking under the table, she saw Tom's hand resting on her mother's leg. She jerked with a start and hit her head on the corner of the table, rattling the glasses. She saw stars for a few seconds.

"Ouch!" she reached up and rubbed her head. The pain brought her shock briefly to an end. Scott reached over and laid his hand on her back.

"You okay, hon?"

"Yes. That was a stupid thing to do," she mumbled. Lily kept rubbing her head and looked at her mother, whose attention had already shifted back to Tom. What was going on? She started to ask her mother just that when Iris looked back at her.

"Do you need some ice for it, dear?" she asked.

"No. I'm fine." Lily drank some of her lemonade and continued to rub her head. "Now, tell me what this is about you selling the house."

Iris looked at Tom and gave him a blushing smile. Scott looked at Lily as if to say: Is this your mother sitting here at the table with us? And Lily thought Tom looked like a lovesick old hound—and he probably still had his hand on her mother's leg. What was going on here?

"Well. . ." her mother started slowly, "we've decided to sell this old place. And Tom's too. Then we're moving to Florida."

"Wha. . .?" Lily started, her eyes wide.

"Sounds great!" enthused Scott. "What brought this about?"

"We got married yesterday," replied Iris, turning to Tom for a quick kiss.

"And I'm taking this lovely lady away to where we can live happily ever after!" Tom said in his lovesick old hound voice.

Lily couldn't move from her seat. She sat stunned, looking at her mother incredulously. She barely heard Scott's enthusiastic congratulations and watched while he stood to shake Tom's hand and give her mother a kiss. Lily continued to sit, transfixed and uncomprehending.

"Married?" she barely spoke the word aloud.

Lily listened in shocked silence as Tom and Iris recounted their last few days. Scott seemed to be enjoying every minute of their account. Lily could hardly bring herself to smile, let alone ask any questions.

"So, how did this come about?" Scott asked, sitting back down.

"You know we've only been seeing one another for a

few weeks. . ." began Tom.

"It's been eighteen days, my love," Iris interjected. He patted her hand in affirmation.

"Eighteen of the best days of my life. But from the first day we both felt like we knew each other for years," he said.

Scott looked over at Lily with a smile, but she continued to stare at her mother and Tom in impassive silence. He turned back to Iris and Tom.

"So you've known each other for eighteen days and got married?" Scott laughed heartily. "This is great! Did you go downtown or what?"

"No. We were helping over at the church for the monthly food distribution and Tom all of a sudden looked at me across the cans of vegetables and said, 'Will you marry me, Iris?' It just seemed the most natural thing in the world for him to ask and me to answer 'yes,' and so I did. I said, 'When?' and he said, 'Today!' "

"After we loaded the last of the food boxes," Tom continued excitedly, "we went to the preacher and I says, 'Would you marry Iris and me, Parson?' And he says, 'If you love Jesus as much as my best deaconess does, I'll be happy to. When?' And I said, 'Is today okay?' He was kinda surprised, you know, and he says again, 'If you love Jesus as much as Iris does, I will.' I told him, 'I love Jesus as much as Iris, Parson. He saved me five years ago and I've been a different man ever since.' He says, 'I'm glad to hear it, Tom.' "

"So we followed him into the sanctuary and the Baileys stood up for us and we were married right then and there!" interjected Iris breathlessly.

"No frills, no planning! We decided today to move to Florida and sell our houses. Tomorrow we're going to get wedding bands and some airline tickets to see what part of Florida looks good to us. We'll rent a car and drive around and when we find something we like, that's where we'll plan to go!"

"What about your jobs?" Lily managed to ask.

"Jobs, schmobs. I quit!" exulted Iris. "Well," she said more quietly with a playful grin, "I gave them notice. But I'm taking my vacation now, so I'm done."

"And my boy can handle our business. It'll be all his when I'm gone anyway. I can stay in touch by computer and fax—fly home every month or so to check things and let you and your mom visit. We'll work out all the details as we go," Tom said airily, winking at his new wife.

"Do all your kids know you and Iris got married, Tom?" Scott asked.

"Nope. You're the first to know—other than the Baileys and the preacher. Whatta ya think?"

"Me?" Scott asked. "I think it's great!"

Tom, Iris, and Scott all looked expectantly at Lily. A few seconds of silence settled around the table and Lily shifted in her chair uncomfortably. She attempted a smile, but was not very successful in the attempt.

"Well, dear. . .?" her mother prompted, her hand holding Tom's more tightly.

"I think it's awful sudden," began Lily. "I mean, you've only known each other a few weeks." She felt something akin to panic rising in her. What had her mother been thinking? They hardly knew this man! She ventured to say so. "You barely know each other. . . ."

"That's the fun of it! We already found out we both like to sleep on the same side of the bed. We almost had our first argument last night!" Tom hugged Iris, who blushed again.

Please, thought Lily, *spare me the details.* She turned to Scott, who seemed to be enjoying the entire discourse. His eyes were merry and he seemed to be sharing a secret with Tom and Iris that didn't include her.

"Young Tom and his family are coming by shortly so we can tell them the good news. We'll call Trisha and Teresa tonight too—they're my girls who live out of town. Iris and I went out and bought a cake and some ice cream today so we could all celebrate tonight."

"You've never bought a cake in your life, Mother," Lily said, her tone sharper than she wanted it to be. If Iris noticed, she didn't let on and only laughed.

"I know! Isn't this wild? Tom's already spoiling me! He said if it's no good we'll just go out to a restaurant and get some dessert!" Iris laughed and turned her sparkling eyes to her husband again. Lily regarded both of them silently, unable to say another word.

Three hours later Scott sat next to Lily in her apartment. Actually, Scott sat by himself for the most part. Lily paced. She would sit next to him briefly, obviously agitated, then busy herself around the apartment. She wiped surfaces that didn't need wiping, she opened curtains only to close them again, and then she would sit down next to Scott for a few minutes, only to jump up again and repeat the same routine. Scott leafed through a book of Lily's, deeming silence his best course until Lily had calmed down somewhat.

"Do you believe this?" Lily finally asked, but he knew better than to answer. "My mother and that. . .man acting like two kids! Kissing on each other and making eyes at each other and. . .wasn't it ridiculous?" She didn't wait for him to answer and Scott did not even attempt a reply. "It was worse than ridiculous! It was ludicrous! What is my mother thinking of? She's married an almost complete stranger! She's never met his kids—except for Tom and his family—and she's talking about moving as far south as she can get!"

Scott quietly watched Lily open the window, close it, and go through the neatly arranged mail on her desk for the third or fourth time. "How could she do this?" she continued. "What was she thinking of?"

"Perhaps," Scott ventured, "she was thinking of herself for a change. Thinking it might be fun to take the first risk she's ever taken. . ."

"By getting married to a man she hardly knows? That's not a risk! It's insanity! He could turn out to be a. . .wife beater or something!"

Scott laid the book aside and went to stand beside Lily. He put his arms around her and felt her trembling. "Hey! Take it easy, princess! Your mom has always been a good judge of character and is an extremely discerning woman."

"She's also been a woman who always plans and weighs things. She's never, ever done anything so. . .so. . .radical in her life! Have you ever seen my mother carry on like that?

Blush like a new bride? Giggle like a little girl?" Lily tried to pull out of Scott's embrace in her agitation, but he held her.

"No, I haven't. I have never seen your mother as happy as she was tonight," he said quietly. Some of the fight seemed to drain from Lily at his soft reply and she slumped against him. Her back to his chest, she gazed out the window and felt the cool night air creep in under the raised window.

"Is that what it was?" she asked, more to herself than Scott.

"Radiantly so, yes. Your mom has been alone for a lot of years, Lily Rose. It's obvious Tom is absolutely smitten with her. He couldn't keep his eyes—"

"Or hands. . ." she interjected, a pout on her face.

". . .off her. She's his wife, my love. Enjoy this with and for her." He touched his lips to her temple. "Why don't you call Tom Junior tomorrow and plan a little reception for them? Before they go to Florida, that is." Scott could sense a change in Lily without looking at her face. She was quiet for the space of several seconds.

"You know, that might not be a bad idea. . . ."

Scott knew that once Lily got an idea or plan of action in mind, it soothed her almost magically. She could bring order back into her life.

He thought again how he hoped he would always be able to cope with her incessant planning and organizing once they were married. He encouraged it now; he wondered if he always would. It would be his life she would be ordering as much as hers someday. He hugged her a little tighter, but Lily was thinking out loud now and clearly oblivious to him.

"Yes, a reception would be so nice. They could meet one another's friends and perhaps stay around here a while longer. Just some light refreshments and the cost would not be too much. . ."

The next day Lily walked into the used machinery shop that Tom owned. She had called before coming to see the younger Tom Donnelly, hoping to enlist his help in planning a reception for their parents. He showed her into his office and Lily wondered if the office of Tom Senior was the same cluttered disarray of papers and invoices that this one was. Tom quickly grabbed a stack of papers from the extra chair in the room and motioned for her to sit down.

"Can I get you a cup of coffee, Lily?" he asked, turning to the coffeepot behind him. The counter's assortment of dirty mugs, old coffee stains, and spilled sugar discouraged Lily from acceptance.

"No, thanks."

Several awkward seconds of silence followed. For reasons she didn't understand, Lily blurted out the first thing that came to her mind. It had nothing to do with her idea for a reception.

"What do you think of our parents' marriage?"

Tom poured himself a cup of coffee and thoughtfully stirred in a couple heaping teaspoons of sugar. He looked at Lily as if he were weighing his response. He sat down in the ragged leather chair and propped his feet up on the desk. Lily began to think he wasn't going to answer her.

"Well," he said finally, "I'll be honest with you, Lily. Your mother seems like a nice lady and all, but this has got to be the most harebrained, ill-conceived, ridiculous thing my father has ever done. Ever since he got into this religion thing a few years back, he's been doing crazy things. But this is the craziest! How long has he known your mother? A week or two? And they get married?" He shook his head and was not smiling.

"It's been almost three weeks," Lily said. "Almost."

"If I'd married Denise three weeks after meeting her, my dad would have had my uh—hide!" he corrected. It wasn't lost on Lily that Tom was adjusting his language for what he thought to be "the religious type." She had surmised that quickly from some of the conversation last night. He put his feet on the floor and leaned on the desk. "Is Iris like this? Jumping into things without any forethought?"

"Not at all. My mother has never done anything rash in her life. I still can't believe this."

"Hmmm. I thought maybe she had put my old man up to this, though I didn't think she seemed the type." He took another loud slurp of his coffee and leaned back. "The deed's done now. They've made their bed and now they've got to sleep in it. We might as well help them celebrate. What did you have in mind for a reception?"

From that first meeting with her new stepbrother, Lily and Tom's wife planned the small reception for the new Mr. and Mrs. Thomas Donnelly. In her usual fashion, Lily was able to continue with her own plans for her and Scott's wedding and

at the same time plan her mother's party. She was adamant—
and young Tom helped her in this—about Iris and Tom staying in town several weeks before going to Florida, and not
putting their houses up for sale until after their trip. Iris, who
had always been the ultimate planner, was no help at all to Lily.
Any question Lily asked was always answered with "Whatever
you think is best, dear," or "That's fine, dear." She would then
turn her attention back to Tom, or to doing something special
for Tom. Scott thought the new Iris was delightful and surprising; Lily found her simply exasperating.

The reception was a success. The weather permitted guests to
circulate inside and outside the house and young Tom's insis-
tence on paying for the food relieved Lily of costs she could
ill afford. She was able to decorate the house with baskets and
vases of fresh flowers and get some special outdoor lighting
for the backyard. Everyone seemed to enjoy the evening,
especially Iris and Tom. Lily had talked her mother into buy-
ing a new dress for the occasion and Tom had worn a suit.
Lily had a corsage made for her mother and Tom was pleased
that his new stepdaughter had gotten him a boutonniere. Lily
had to admit they made the handsomest couple at the party.
And the happiest. She thought again how she had never seen
her mother so happy. She almost envied her.

   After all the guests had left, Iris and Lily set about gathering up the dishes. Tom and Scott finished loading a few
remaining chairs from the church into Scott's truck. The
two men sat down in lawn chairs in the backyard, both

with loosened ties, their suit coats off, and their shirtsleeves rolled up.

"This was really nice of Lily," said Tom. "I'm glad I got to meet some of Iris's friends. It was worth putting off our honeymoon for a little while longer. I think I had one piece of cake too many, though," he said good-naturedly, rubbing his stomach, which hung well over his belt.

"You'll run it off in Florida," Scott said, wadding up a paper cup and throwing it into an open trash can. The two men sat in silence briefly, the quiet talking of Iris and Lily drifting to them from the kitchen.

"Lily's not much like her mother, is she?" Tom asked.

Scott chuckled quietly and shook his head. "Several weeks back I would have told you she's exactly like her mother. And she is—at least, she's exactly like her mother used to be. Iris was even more methodical than Lily, if you can believe it. But you came along and all that changed."

"Not all of it. Iris can't let a dirty dish sit in the sink for five minutes, let alone overnight. She don't tolerate bein' late for anything. And she has organized my closets and drawers so much that I feel like I'm messing them up when I pull out a pair of socks to wear!" Scott nodded in understanding. "But," he continued, "if I suggest we take a walk or run up to the lake to take the boat out, she's all for it."

Scott looked at Tom thoughtfully. "How did you do it?" he asked.

"Do what?"

"Get Iris to do the spontaneous and unpredictable." Scott changed position and studied Tom. "Lily is organized to the nth degree. But Iris was the same way. If I suggest, oh, like I did the other day, 'let's take a swim,' Lily gives me one of her disgusted looks and reminds me of the other things we're supposed to be doing. It's like she's paranoid about any spur-of-the-moment adventure. I don't know if I'm going to be able to live like that the rest of my life." Scott surprised himself; he had never thought Lily's incessant attention to detail bothered him so much. He said so to Tom.

"You know, I don't think Lily's obsessive compulsion ever bothered me until I saw the change in Iris. Iris and Lily have always been content, busy women. In the last few weeks I've seen Iris laugh—really laugh! I've heard Iris giggle like a kid being tickled. Lily and I have dated for over two years. I've never known her to laugh like that—and 'giggle. . . .' " He hesitated and smiled a small smile. " 'Giggle' is as foreign to my sweet Lily as a weekly planner is to me." As if to confirm what he said, they heard Iris's laughter come from the kitchen and both looked to see Lily smiling at her mother in her quiet way. "I would love to hear Lily laugh," he said quietly.

"Is Lily unhappy?" Tom asked, removing his tie with a sigh of pleasure.

"No, not unhappy. She's just different from me. When I guffaw—and you've probably noticed I guffaw a lot—Lily just smiles sweetly. She sometimes chuckles quietly, but that's about it. I guess she just doesn't ever. . .let herself go?" He shook his head with one of his own chuckles. "That wouldn't even be Lily. What am I saying?"

"Maybe you. . .shouldn't give her the option," Tom ventured.

"What do you mean?"

"Take the initiative on something and don't let her talk you out of it. Maybe throw her into the pool instead of asking her to go for a swim."

Scott shook his head. "I don't think something like that would be a good idea. . . ." he said. Tom scratched his head and the two of them were quiet with their own thoughts for a minute.

"Maybe you should try something that you know she would probably really like, but would never try on her own. Something that would catch her off guard, but would intrigue her so much that she would be glad for the change of plans."

"I don't know of anything—wait a minute!" Scott snapped his fingers. "I've got it!"

"Tell me," said Tom.

"Not a chance," Scott said, grinning. "You'll have to wait for our wedding to see it. Yep, I've got the perfect thing. If I can get us to October 15th without me burning her daily calendar, I've got it."

"If you wait for your wedding day, you may find you've waited too long," warned Tom. Scott laughed and stood.

"Look who's sounding the alarm! The man who meets a woman one day and marries her three weeks later! Trust me on this one, Tom. You've given me an idea, and your wife has given me the inspiration. I'll trust the Lord to keep me from going overboard."

So from that one conversation on the night of Iris and Tom's reception, Scott made his plans. He almost failed in his careful scheming on numerous occasions: a few hours shooting baskets with his young friends, or sleeping in on Saturdays, would entice him from the tasks at hand. But his hours in the company of his fiancée had had their effect on him. He began to plan some of his days in advance. He didn't carry a calendar or checklist, but he would mentally tackle certain days with a clear plan of action. Never one to care much about the weather, Scott now prayed earnestly about their wedding day. He couldn't recall the weather conditions for any of their friends' weddings. He never considered it important. But for Lily, he considered it important. He wanted to make one thing perfectly clear when they got married, and he needed the cooperation of the weather to make his point.

October 15th arrived, the perfect day for a wedding. Scott looked out on the morning with a spontaneous whoop. The air was still with only the slightest hint of a breeze. A few clouds accented the deep blue of the mid-autumn sky. The changing colors of the trees were at their peak and the air was saturated with the heady, robust fragrance of fall. He gave Lily a call at her grandmother's, where she had spent the night. She was adamant about not seeing Scott before the wedding. He thought it a silly old wives' tale, but he knew sometimes the silly things were important to Lily.

"Good morning, princess," he said when she came to the telephone. "Haven't changed your mind, have you?"

"No, Scott. Have you?"

"Not a chance. I suppose you've been up since cockcrow?" he asked, rummaging in the refrigerator for something to eat.

"No. I slept in this morning—didn't get up until seven. Are you ready?"

"Never been readier. I'll see you at church in a few hours, my flower. Call me if you need anything." He hung up and proceeded to pull out some leftover pizza from a few nights ago. He whistled as he set the pizza in the microwave oven. He knew their wedding day was going to be great!

Meanwhile, Lily resumed her place at the table with her mother, Tom, and her grandparents. She had little appetite and pushed her eggs around distractedly. She missed the smile that passed between her mother and grandmother.

"I had better get to the beautician's to get my hair and nails done," she said.

"Are you still thinking of having your hair done up?" asked her mother, finishing the last of her coffee.

"Of course. What other way would I have it done?" Lily gave up trying to eat and removed her plate and her mother's from the table.

"You should wear it down. Have it gently curled. I could even do it for you."

"Down? Wear my hair down? Are you serious?" Lily was about to state her arguments when her mother cut her off.

"Haven't you ever noticed how much Scott remarks about your hair when you don't pin it up or French braid it? Why don't you fix it just for him? It would surprise and delight him," Iris said, helping gather the dishes.

"But it's not the fashion right now, Mom."

"So what? You're not marrying the editor of some fashion magazine! You're marrying Scott. I know I've heard him say numerous times: 'Why don't you wear your hair down, *princess*?' " she emphasized the last word with a teasing smile.

Lily turned to her grandfather. "What do you think, Papa?"

"I like the boy. Do what you think he would like."

Lily saw her reflection in the kitchen window. Perhaps this once. . . .

Several hours later, Lily Rose Blackstone walked the aisle on the arm of her grandfather. The delicate simplicity of her bridal gown and the pearl and sapphire necklace that graced her neck created a look of gentle elegance. Her hair cascaded about her shoulders and down her back with a small curl of hair brought back and gathered with blue ribbons and a white gardenia on the crown of her head. She blushed with pleasure at Scott's surprised smile and thought he had never looked so appealing: tall, tanned, his face full of love for her. When her grandfather placed her hand in Scott's, Scott silently mouthed "I love you" to her and squeezed her hand. They spoke their vows with solemnity and love before God and to each other. Lily sought to fix every detail of the ceremony in her mind. Scott's kiss was tender and sweet. She returned it with an ardor born of the knowledge that she was now his.

Amid the kisses, tears, and congratulations of their parents, grandparents, and the wedding party at the back of the church, Scott quickly pulled Lily into his embrace once more before their guests came through the receiving line.

"You are beautiful, Lily Rose Ferguson," he whispered

against her lips. Lily liked the sound of her new name and thrilled again to Scott's touch. She hoped everything at the reception would go as smoothly as things did at the wedding. She had trusted the business with the cars and a limousine to Scott; she only hoped now she wouldn't be sorry she had. She knew Scott was almost hopelessly disorganized and a deplorable planner. She couldn't resist asking him two quick questions.

"Is everything all set with the cars? Did the guys get the decorations on them?"

"Don't worry, Rosie. I took care of everything," he answered. They both turned their attention to their guests and for the next half hour happily received well wishes and congratulations.

Lily had arranged for only a few photographs to be taken after the ceremony. They would have time to load their traveling clothes in Scott's car after the traditional drive around the neighborhood and before the reception. She had planned an early reception with a dinner so she and Scott could leave at a fairly early hour and drive an hour to the hotel where she had made reservations for their first night together. They would then start for Maine in the morning and spend a short week in the northeastern part of the country.

"Come on, princess," said Scott, taking her hand after the final picture had been taken.

They went to the church foyer and Lily was shocked to find no one standing outside to throw the sachets of birdseed she and her bridesmaids had so painstakingly assembled. Their maid of honor and best man had already gotten into the car—which was not decorated—and encouraged them to hurry.

"What is going on?" asked Lily, turning to Scott, who helped her into the car.

"You're about to see. Take us to our rendezvous point, driver," he said to his grinning best man. "And no spying on us." He silenced Lily's questions with a lingering kiss. In a few minutes they had pulled into a park just outside the city limits.

"I want you to know we may not have a perfectly managed marriage, my love. You can't be afraid of the unexpected—even if it's unexpected only for you. You can't plan every moment of every day. You're going to need to cut yourself—and me—some slack on occasion. This is the first of many surprises for you. You'd better get used to them." He opened the door and got out of the car, holding his hand out to Lily. She looked at him timidly and carefully lifted her skirts as she stepped out of the car. "We'll see you guys in a few minutes," Scott said to their best man and maid of honor. "Come, my princess," he said to Lily, steering her towards a gravel walking trail.

Lily's maid of honor, Cyndy, gathered Lily's short train up for her and looped it over her arm. She gave Lily a kiss on the cheek. "See you in a little while, Lil," she said with a wink at Scott and walked away.

"Scott, what is—"

"We're going to have our first private discussion as man and wife, Lily, and I wanted to have it privately, unhurried, but immediately. Smells great out here, doesn't it?" he asked.

"Wonderful. But we need to get to the reception."

"Not yet we don't." He pulled her into his embrace.

"Scott, we can't keep our guests waiting," she said, but returned his kiss eagerly. Scott kissed her several more times, leaving Lily feeling surprised at the intensity of her own passion. He smiled at her and pulled her gently to walk close beside him again.

"We cannot have every minute of our lives planned out, dear one. So, I thought I would make that clear from the start. We are not going to stay at the hotel you picked out for tonight and we are not going to Maine."

"Where are we going?" Lily asked, a sinking feeling of dread quickly replacing her short-lived passion. All her carefully laid plans had been pushed aside.

"To Chicago. I've got tickets for a stage play, tickets for a football game—sorry, sweetheart, I couldn't resist—and some great eating planned. We can do Maine next fall."

"What about tonight?" she asked, walking along quietly beside him.

"We'll find a spot. I've got a couple in mind. I don't want any surprise nighttime visitors—and that's just what happens when you've prearranged a hotel stay. Trust me, my love; we won't sleep in the car."

"Here they come!" Lily heard someone shout. She looked up at the clearing ahead and saw what had to be the entire contingent of guests from their wedding ceremony.

"What—?" she started, but never finished. Scott pulled her into a short run. The birdseed, laughingly tossed by their family and friends, rained around and on them.

"Here we are, my bride!" Scott announced and Lily stared openmouthed at the colorful hot air balloon before them. "This is our ride to the reception," Scott explained. "And why we're taking a shorter, cheaper honeymoon. What do you think? Are you game?"

Lily had nothing to say, but her wide eyes and amazed smile were all the encouragement Scott needed. They climbed into the balloon's basket with Cyndy handing Lily her bouquet and Alan handing Scott two glasses and a bottle of sparkling cider. Everyone clapped, cheered, and took pictures as the balloonist gave the two of them some brief instructions. In minutes they were rising lightly, amazingly, gloriously off the ground. Scott had his reward: Lily squealed with delight and held tightly to him, her face radiantly happy. They waved to their wedding guests and continued to rise higher. The landscape broadened into a dazzling display of colors. Scott could little relish his new bride's delight, he was so enthralled by the experience himself.

"Is this a rush or what?" he said to their pilot. The middle-aged man gave him a big grin.

"It never gets old!"

"Scott, look!" Lily pointed to a sparkling river that wound its way through the countryside. They could not get enough of the scenery or the thrill of floating over the brilliant hues of sun-drenched colors, the reds, golds, and oranges of autumn. The entire trip was less than an hour, but Scott was glad he had planned it. And he thanked God again for the perfect day.

As they began their descent to a field adjacent to the reception hall, Scott pulled Lily closer to him. "Well, my flower, this is the reason for your cheaper honeymoon. It's also your wedding gift. Not disappointed, are you?"

"Disappointed?! How could I be? This has been the biggest thrill of my life!" Lily declared.

"No," Scott said into her ear. "That's yet to come—tonight. . . ."

And Lily laughed.

It was not a laugh of derision or nervousness. It was laughter that rang with delight. It was the lilting laughter of a new bride, thrilled to belong to someone in a totally new way and secure in the love she knew he had only for her. The slightest blush touched her cheeks and the love in Lily's eyes thrilled Scott.

"I love you, darling. It's been a wonderful beginning for our life together—even if it wasn't what I had planned." Scott pressed her fingertips to his lips. Lily had never called him by any term of endearment before; she had always called him by his name. He hoped this too was something new, but permanent, in their marriage.

He hoped they would never tire of surprising each other in little ways. He hoped their lives would be full of love and laughter. He hoped for children to fill their home.

For the moment, however, he hoped he would remember to go back for the theater tickets he had forgotten to pack.

CHAPTER 2

Twilight

Lying on his flabby belly, Jack relished the penetrating warmth of the sun on his back. He wished he could rest or sleep in the sun all the time. At night he was always so cold, and the moon's soft glow offered no warmth like its daytime counterpart. Its light was no rival for the brightness of the sun either; it was no help to his dimming vision. He often sought the heat that poured out from the floor vent, but even it did not have the satisfying, permeating heat of the wonderful orb of the day. He rolled to his side and squeezed his eyelids more tightly against the harsh brightness—harsh even to his dim, old eyes.

He thought about looking for that gopher again. The varmint kept getting into Gordon's garden. Jack and Gordon had been companions for more years than Jack could count. Gordon was bigger than him, weighed more than him, but Jack felt himself to be the protector of their shared home and even Gordon himself. Jack cared little for the garden or what Gordon grew in it, but he thought he should be the one to ferret out the gopher. Gordon really enjoyed that silly vegetable garden. But that gopher. That gopher was a pest and kept disrupting their otherwise quiet existence. If it wasn't helping itself to what was rightfully Gordon's, the annoying creature was making tunnels. The softened, ragged mounds of dirt often caused Gordon to lose his already-shaky footing. Jack felt it was his job to get rid of that gopher once and for all. That gopher was a smart one, though. And he was quick. Many a time Jack almost had him, but he would always just get away, disappearing into the rich, dark earth. He would get that gopher for Gordon. Gordon was his best friend and this was something he could still do for him. He would still go fishing with Gordon, rarely, but Jack had not been out hunting with Gordon for many seasons. He missed those times. . . just the two of them out hunting ducks or rabbits. But hunting was demanding and a lot of work. It took a lot of energy. And Jack didn't have enough energy anymore. Ah, but it was a sweet memory: just the two of them—even Ruby didn't come along. It was good companionship, good exercise, and plain good times. *Yep, those were the days,* he thought, rolling to his other side a little stiffly.

It was so quiet around the homestead lately. It seemed the birds didn't even sing much. He used to hear Gordon whistling all the time, but that had ceased too. Peculiar. He stretched briefly. The sun felt so good. Maybe if he remained stretched out here just a little while longer he would be able to get up and get after that gopher that had been pestering Gordon lately and getting into his garden. He didn't care for the garden himself, or for what grew there, but there was this gopher. . .

Ruby looked down at Jack from her favorite place on the porch. Old Jack was getting really old, that was for sure. They used to have races every day, she and Jack. She would beat him occasionally, but their best races were the ones that ended in a tie. They would argue for the rest of the day over who beat whom "by a nose." But now Jack complained of his aching bones and it had been more days than she could remember since they had had one of their races. She brushed a pesky fly away from her face. The only racing they did now was to see who would fall asleep first. She could never stay awake long enough to see who won those races.

"Well, Rube," Jack would say with some of the former glint in his rheumy old eyes, "who won that one?" Every morning he asked her the same question. Every morning she gave him the same answer.

"I did, of course, you old dog you. You know I'm the fastest at everything around here. I'm the 'woman of the house,' as Gordon says and there's just a lot of things you can't beat me at." And they would snicker at their timeworn barbs as if they were exchanging them for the first time.

Ruby yawned and ran her tongue over her almost useless teeth. What few teeth she had left didn't do her much good. They were weak and yellow with age. She had given up trying to eat crunchy food long ago; it was just too much work and made her few remaining teeth hurt. The last time she had tried a crunchy snack her final swallow alerted her that some of the extra crunch in the last bite had been one of her teeth. She didn't care for a repeat of that. There was one advantage to swearing off those crunchy treats, however:

nobody could call her "Fat Ruby" anymore. "Fat" hardly described her skinny frame, ribs protruding out her sides. In fact, "Ruby" hardly described her anymore either. Most of her red was gray now.

Where had all the time gone between every tom in the neighborhood wanting to be in her company to the gray, essentially toothless old hag that now sat between old gray Gordon and tired old Jack? *No one howls about my good looks anymore,* she thought ruefully. But, it was all right. Gordon loved her; he was as affectionate as always. And Jack, in his own way, loved her too, she supposed. And she loved him too, she guessed, but not like she loved Gordon. She still loved Gordon passionately as she did when she was young with her ruby red hair and big eyes.

My, she remembered when Gordon would watch the two of them race: just her and Jack. They had some fine races back then. It was back before Jack complained of old age and aching bones. . . .

Gordon looked out the window at his dearly loved companions as he finished up the remaining dishes. *Poor old Jack can no longer spot a barn at fifty feet, much less a rabbit,* he thought with a cluck of his tongue. He couldn't hear for beans either. Gordon would have to shout to be heard. Even then Jack was slow to respond, like he wasn't sure he'd heard correctly. *Well, Jack doesn't have the benefit of a hearing aid and bifocals like I do,* he thought with a weak smile. And Ruby was a neat old gal: never demanding, never giving him any trouble. She would often look at him lovingly through her gentle eyes, content to feel his gnarled old hand on her or just be near him. She hadn't always been faithful to him, it was true. Years ago she would leave for two or three days at a stretch. She gave no hints she was leaving, they'd just get up in the morning and she would be gone. At first, Gordon would worry. But she came home again. Every time. He had stopped worrying or concerning himself about her days away long ago. Neither he nor Jack felt the need to know where she'd been. She would just come back and they would slip into their same routine as if she had never left. If Jack disapproved of her meandering, he never let on to Gordon.

Of course, sometimes it was Gordon and Jack who would go off for a few days. Generally the two of them would go on an overnight camping and fishing trip or do some serious hunting. The fond memory brought a smile to his lined face. The two of them had never sought to find out where Ruby went on her short excursions and she apparently wasn't bothered by their occasional jaunts. Not infrequently, however, she would give them the proverbial cold shoulder for the better part of a day when they first returned. By the time evening came, the three of them would be contentedly resting in the living room. Gordon would turn on the television sometimes, but generally he would read his Bible and talk to his God.

Gordon dried his freckled hands after the last pan was washed, rinsed, and set to drip-dry. He should go check the garden and grab his .22 rifle just in case he spotted the gopher. On second thought, he decided the gopher wasn't worth the bother; he grabbed his favorite old ball cap instead and stepped outside into the waning afternoon sunshine. He reached for his cane, which rested in its usual spot next to the door. With slow, halting steps, he descended the two steps. The stairs creaked under his weight and he thought again how he ought to fix them. He pushed a loose chunk of paint free with the end of his cane. He should paint them too. But the rheumatism was taking its toll on his eighty-seven-year-old frame, and tasks like step repair didn't come easy as they once had.

He walked slowly to the garden, his back bent and his left foot dragging slightly. Ruby and Jack fell into step with him. There was no conversation. Like so much else, their daily pattern of living came as naturally as breathing and their communication needed no words. *The garden is doing well this summer,* thought Gordon. No recent sign of the gopher or any rabbits. He used the tip of his cane to break up the earth around one of his tomato plants. The tomatoes would be ripe enough for picking starting next week. He would eat a few probably and put the rest out on a table in the front yard with a sign reading: "free."

"Well, Rube, Jack, let's be goin' in for the night. The sun will be settin' before too long."

So go they did: the elderly man lumbering along with the help of his cane, the old dog already missing the full sun of day, and the aged, graying barn cat following last of all.

CHAPTER 3

Legacy

For the third time in as many days, Gwen pulled into the hospital parking lot. The daily trips to the hospital were more of a chore than the daily care her mother-in-law had needed during the past ten months. Gwen shook her head with a sigh. Ten long months had passed since Florence's cancer had been diagnosed and she had moved in with them. Gwen loved her mother-in-law, but now she wondered if their joint decision to have Tim's elderly mother live with them had been a wise one. The doctor had said the cancer would claim Florence in three or "at the absolute most, six months." Now that it had been over ten months, Florence seemed no worse or better. . .until this fall.

Why, Gwen asked herself, *does Florence insist on doing things she can no longer do?* Whatever possessed her to try to take down the curtains for washing? As far as she was concerned, the curtains didn't need washing in the first place!

Gwen scolded herself for her anger, again, but she was just so tired. Her days had become a monotonous, exhausting routine: get Tim off to work, get the kids off to school,

grab a second cup of coffee. Next, she would help Florence
to the bathroom, get her breakfast—if she would eat—then
bathed, and dressed. Then Gwen would try to do laundry,
dishes, or the cleaning before Sarabeth bounded in with at
least one friend in tow. Her afternoons were a blur of ban-
daging banged-up knees while listening simultaneously to
Florence's endless chatter. Trips to the doctor or the pharmacy, not to mention the stacks of medical forms she was
forever trying to make sense of, filled any spare minutes she
might have. After three o'clock the rest of the kids would
come home: Nick would have some kind of ball practice,
Jolee, either piano or ballet lessons, and Debbie, a new crisis
with a boyfriend, or cheerleading practice. Tim might (or
might not) be home in time for supper. From there? From
there things usually deteriorated.

Now this. Florence with a broken hip. More medical
forms. Hours at the hospital with a million things to do at
home. Trying to find a sitter for Sarabeth in the afternoons.
Gwen sighed again on her way to Florence's room. *Lord,* she
thought, *will this ever end?* She prayed again for a better attitude, not really believing it possible, and took one more deep
breath before she entered Florence's room. She put on her
best smile.

"Hi, Mom," she said, giving her mother-in-law a quick
kiss. She sat on a chair, ready for the list of complaints she
knew she was about to hear. "Did you sleep well last night?"

"Sleep!" Florence raised her thin, bruised hand for
emphasis. "How can a body sleep in a place like this? Six different nurses tried to start this IV again before one of them

finally got it and that old biddy over there carried on all night!" She pointed a shaking finger at the sleeping woman across the room. "Of course, now she sleeps!" She stopped to drop her hand and catch her breath. "Has that young upstart that calls himself a doctor told you anything? He never gives me a straight answer. Just pats my hand like he was patting an old dog on the head. I'd like to take a switch to his better side!" Her tirade left her winded and she fell back against her pillows.

"I haven't seen the doctor, Mom. I'll have Tim call him." Gwen remembered meeting the orthopedic specialist when Florence was admitted. She agreed; he had appeared young and full of himself.

"Are you having any pain? Can I get you anything?" The questions were automatic and Gwen hardly looked up. Instead, she began clearing crumpled leaves and wilted petals that had fallen on the bedside table from the flowers that now drooped over the edge of the vase. *These flowers look like I feel,* Gwen thought to herself. Unknown to her, Florence watched her daughter-in-law clear away the fallen petals without a word. Gwen wondered what she would make for supper tonight; she had forgotten to set any meat out to thaw. She suddenly realized she'd been miles away mentally from her mother-in-law.

"I'm sorry, Mom. What did you say?" she looked up after pushing the brown, curled petals into the wastebasket, and turned her attention back to Florence.

"I didn't say anything, Gwendolyn," Florence replied quietly. Gwen could feel her face reddening, but Florence patted her arm with a tired smile. "For a change," she finished.

"I'm sorry, Mom. I'm a little distracted today."

"I know these last ten months have been hard for you, Gwendolyn. I'm not so old or blind that I don't see the dark circles under your eyes or hear your tired sighs. I know too that I rattle on nonstop most days." She paused before continuing. "Perhaps it's time we checked into one of those old folks' homes—"

"No, Mom. We're in this together, remember? Tim, you, and I decided that at the start." Gwen found herself defending the very thing she was less sure of only minutes ago. Yet, hearing her mother-in-law say it made it seem so. . . so something. She couldn't put a word on it. She reached over and brushed a strand of wiry, white hair away from Florence's mouth. She regarded her mother-in-law intently.

"I'm that transparent, huh?" She didn't wait for an answer. "This is harder for you, Mom. You're the one who had to give up your home, who has the cancer, and now has the broken hip. And you get the brunt of my worst days, too." She leaned back in her chair with a sigh.

"Well, you 'get the brunt,' as you say, of my worst days as well, so I guess we're even." Florence was quiet for the space of a few seconds and looked out the window across the room. "Sometimes I do think it would be better for all of us—if I went to one of those places, I mean. But there have been so many good things for me while living with you and the family."

Gwen watched Florence quietly, grateful for the opportunity to just sit for a few minutes. Florence changed her position slightly and continued.

"You never knew my sister Molly because she died young. But our Sarabeth is so like her! It's uncanny how much her giggling sounds like Molly's did!" Her eyes twinkled with the memory, but her voice was edged with a sadness born over many years. "Sometimes it's like I'm eight years old again, playing with my little sister. . ." She waved the IV'd hand at Gwen. "And that Nick! When he comes bounding through that door, it's my little Timmy I see again! But he always brings me right back to the present. Whether I bawl him out or encourage him to do something, he always says the same thing." She stuck her nose up in the air and rolled her head back slightly. Gwen had to snicker at how much she looked like Nick when she did it. " 'Aw, Gram,' he says, 'you sound just like Mom.' " She chuckled to herself and said quietly to Gwen, "I take it as a compliment."

Gwen blushed at the kind words and leaned back in her chair as Florence returned her gaze to the view through the hospital window. *There are,* Gwen thought, *treasured moments between the insurance forms and the cleaning.* She recalled the day Florence painstakingly put together a bonnet for Sarabeth's doll from material Gwen was throwing away once she had converted a too-short pair of pants into shorts for Sara. She remembered the night Debbie had grilled her grandmother with dozens of questions that dated back "to when you lived, Grandma," as she had so tactlessly put it. Gwen smiled to herself. What Deb learned that night was probably far more than she learned in her history class on that era. Yet some of their best times were between just the two of them: she and Florence. Gwen had a better understanding of Tim now than she ever had. Her mother-in-law had given her rare glimpses of the little boy and then the teenager who had become the man Gwen married.

Yes, she sighed, *we do have our bad days.* Really bad days. But tucked in between the folds of monotony and weary routine were bright, sparkling threads. Lessons. Laughter. Love.

"We have had our good days, haven't we, Mom? Thank you for the reminder." Gwen turned to her mother-in-law with a grateful smile. But Florence was asleep, her lips slightly parted, her eyeglasses magnifying the wrinkled skin of her eyelids. Gwen started to leave, knowing the older children would soon be home with places to go and stories of the day to tell. Yet she hesitated and sat down again, looking at the elderly woman beside her.

"I can stay a few more minutes, Mom," she whispered, placing her hand tenderly on Florence's fragile, bruised one. She touched the worn gold wedding band on her mother-in-law's ring finger and looked lovingly on the face of the woman with whom she shared her home and family. "You have more to teach me. . .and God knows I have more to learn."

CHAPTER 4

Full Circle

Her four words hung in the air like the faint fragrance of a candle snuffed out by a deft pinch of the wick.

"I called Dad today," were the words nineteen-year-old Taylor had spoken quietly from her half-sitting, half-sprawled position on the living room sofa. Ursula was sure her face showed unmasked surprise, if not absolute shock. She suddenly felt the need to sit down and did so.

"What do you think, Mom? Even though I'm sure I shocked the socks off him, I think Dad was glad to hear from me—glad that I made what I think was a long-overdue contact. He even invited me to visit him over spring break!"

Ursula heard what Taylor said, but it seemed her words came to her from another room or even another planet. Taylor had called her father. Ursula knew that someday Taylor would want to get in touch with or meet her father, but now that "someday" was here she felt unprepared for it. Totally unprepared for it.

She and Arnie had divorced when Taylor was barely a toddler. Arnie felt a wife and child "tied him down too much."

That marriage and fatherhood were not what he really wanted, after all. Soon after the divorce he had moved halfway across the country and then around the world. As a career military man, he never stayed in one place for long. Not in the short time he and Ursula had been married nor, presumably, once he was free of them. He had sent money for a while, even an occasional note asking about Taylor as she grew up without him. But all that had stopped years ago, almost two decades ago. Ursula had long since stopped looking for any word—or money—from Arnie. She had set about managing their lives without him. Any anger or bitterness she might have had, she had put behind her by the time Taylor entered grade school. With prayer, diligence, hard work, and a "never look back" attitude, she had gotten a good job, bought a nice house, and reared her daughter alone, but joyfully. Taylor had always given her more laughter than tears or trials. She was well-adjusted, happy, athletic, and popular. She communicated openly and honestly with her; they were friends as well as family. *Perhaps,* Ursula thought, *I should have been expecting a lot of changes as Taylor began to make her own way in the world.* She had already been away at college for one year and another was about to start. Well, she had been ready for a lot of changes. But not this one. Not now.

"Tell me again how all this came about," she said, her attention coming back to the present and to her long-legged daughter who had taken to twirling a strand of black hair around one of her fingers.

"Late yesterday before you got home from work,"

Taylor said casually. "Even though Dad has never called or anything, I've had this persistent desire to meet him all of a sudden. It's been like a passion with me!" she exclaimed, spreading her arms for emphasis.

"I mean," she said with a sheepish grin and a quieter tone, "I have never been able to remember him at all. I've seen the pictures you have in the albums in the basement, but. . .well, haven't you at least wondered what he looks like from time to time? Is he bald? Is he paunchy? Does he wear bifocals? Did he remarry?"

Ursula started to shake her head. She had not wondered nor thought about Arnie for a long time. Or, if she had, she quickly dismissed any thought of him. She figured it was a waste of time and energy, both of which she conserved as much as possible in her busy schedule. But Taylor did not give her time to respond.

"He said he was sorry he's never called or written, but the more time that passed, he felt he shouldn't 'intrude' into our lives. I personally thought that was a little weird," she interjected. "After all, I am (I found out) still his only daughter. Be that as it may, I want to get to know him and told him so."

"I'm sure you did," Ursula smiled with a knowing nod of her head. "Just how did you track him down?" she asked.

"I made at least a dozen calls to the navy, which is a story in itself, but I finally was able to locate him in Florida. You know, it would be so perfect to go down there on spring break with Trish and Ruth! We wouldn't stay with Dad, but I could spend as little or as much time with him as I wanted. Anyway," she paused before continuing and her tone became more serious. "My psych course last semester really made me start thinking about Dad: what he's like, how much I'm like him. . .things like that. You understand how I feel, don't you, Mom?"

"Yes, I think I can a little. . ." her response was shortened by the ringing of the telephone in her daughter's room.

"Hold that thought, Mom; it's probably Dan on the phone. I'll be right back. . . ." Taylor sprinted down the hall to her room, leaving Ursula to her own thoughts. Ursula swallowed the last of her tea and looked out the window.

Did she understand how Taylor felt? In a way she supposed she did. She was a teenager when she learned, quite by accident, that she had been adopted by her parents. She had needed closure, as Taylor would call it, once she knew she had been adopted. It had taken years, but she had finally learned of her roots. So, yes, she could understand why Taylor needed to meet her father.

Father. He sired Taylor, she thought angrily. *He never fathered her.*

Ah! Given the opportunity, bitterness was quick to raise its ugly head. Ursula bowed her head and asked forgiveness for her caustic thought as quickly as it had come to her. After almost twenty years she would not give into anger so easily. It was futile. It was wrong. It brought no healing or help. And this was not about her or her and Arnie. It was about Taylor and Arnie. It was about a relationship that Taylor obviously and understandably wanted to build with her father. A relationship that Taylor needed to build with her father.

"Thank You, Lord," she said quietly, "for reminding me

what is important now for Taylor and her dad."

"So, what do you think?" Taylor asked as she came back into the room.

"I think you need to meet your dad. It's long overdue. It's time for you to get to know the man who gave you your stubborn streak and long legs!"

"I know the long legs didn't come from you, Shorty," Taylor laughed. "But the stubbornness may be up for grabs!" She reached for the nail file she had been using earlier. She looked up at Ursula with an expression that matched her now-serious tone. "Are you sure it's okay with you if I go to Florida? Skeletons in the closet and that sort of thing won't. . ."

Ursula cut her off with a wave of her hand and went to the kitchen.

"Don't be silly. You should do this, Taylor. It will be good for your father, too. But tell me more about your telephone conversation. You probably about gave the man a heart attack when you called him!"

Taylor followed her mother into the kitchen, blowing at her fingertips and putting the nail file away. She reached for an apple from the basket on the table and munched reflectively before answering.

"I probably did. Well, he didn't say anything for almost a full minute. I wondered if he had just hung up. Then he started in with the apology, like I told you. And then, well, he may have started crying, Mom. His voice sounded a little strained. I don't know him well enough to know, though. It was probably more of an emotional moment for him than me. I mean, I had been planning this and going over it in my mind for weeks—maybe months. Then he started asking me questions rapid-fire: What was I interested in? Did I work? Did I go to school? Do I have a boyfriend?—that sort of thing. He really didn't give me a chance to ask about him, now that I think of it. He did ask about you too, Mom," she concluded with a raise of her eyebrows.

I would guess that to be the natural—and polite—thing to do, Ursula thought to herself.

"In fact," Taylor continued, picking up her narrative, "His exact words were: 'Is your mother as foxy as she was twenty years ago?' "

Ursula gave Taylor a skeptical smile, but her daughter pointed at her with her partially eaten apple in hand. " 'No,' I said to him, 'she's foxier than she was twenty years ago!' "

Taylor gave her mother a quick kiss on the cheek. "You owe me one, Mom. We can talk more about this tomorrow, if you want. I've got to go get ready for Daniel." She left the kitchen and walked back to her room.

Ursula looked after her with a smile and a contented sigh. She was glad that this time had finally come. Perhaps it had always been closer to the edge of her consciousness than she was ready to admit. Taylor and Dan might well be headed for the altar in another year or two. It was obvious to Ursula that Dan very much loved her daughter and that Taylor was equally taken with him. Dan had already finished graduate school and had a good position in his company; she half expected Taylor would get an engagement ring soon. That would mean a wedding. The wedding would mean Arnie's return, she hoped, to give away his daughter. In spite of the years and the total lack of communication, she knew it would be what Taylor wanted. She wanted it too. More for Taylor than anything else. She would be content with that, no matter what her own emotions in all of it might be.

What a spring break this will be for you, Arnie, she thought. *Get ready for my. . .no, OUR little girl. She's very much a woman now. This will be your time to catch up. Your time to get to know your daughter and her to know you.* Ursula picked up an apple and took a big bite. *And a time for her to better know herself.*

CHAPTER 5

And Seven Makes Two

This was where it had all begun. Agatha Farnsworth sat down contentedly in a chair near the entrance to her church's Family Center. She looked around her approvingly. Finally, they were in their new church facility. She had fond memories of the first Vineyard Fellowship Church, but none of them included the brown-tiled floor and browner-still countertops where she and other women of the church had prepared funeral luncheons, women's teas, and fellowship meals. No, she would never miss that old kitchen! At her age she would not be spending much time in the new kitchen nor, she thought with a private grin, making use of the basketball hoops overhead. Just the same, she appreciated the new facilities and was delighted with the adjacent sanctuary.

She was so excited about this weekend! They were having a grand two-day event commemorating the opening of the new Vineyard Fellowship Church of Jesus Christ, but her own excitement had little to do with the structure around her. Most of her final children's Sunday school class would be here today at her invitation. Twenty years ago, at the age of fifty, she had taught her last Sunday school class. Her entire class of seven-year-olds included two boys and five girls. She and her husband, Phillip, had lovingly nicknamed this last class "The Seven." Aggy had been able to locate each of those now-grown children by mail, telephone, or E-mail. All but two would be here this weekend and she and Phillip could not be happier. Between nods and greetings to others who were coming early, Aggy thought back to that memorable 1975. . . .

So much had happened that year! She met her dear, loving Phillip that year. She met her final class of Sunday school students that September. Best of all, she had met Jesus Christ that year.

Her last position as a nanny was with the children of Benjamin and Carletta Farnsworth. By that time, Aggy had been a nanny for a half dozen families in her thirty-year career. The Farnsworth girls had proven to be a fitting end to her vocation. They had been easy to care for and their parents were kind and generous to her. She had met Phillip Farnsworth when he had come over unannounced to his brother's in early March. Aggy was the only person in the house at the time. She smiled at the memory. She probably would have fallen in love with Phillip that very day if their first encounter hadn't been so unusual.

Their conversation had begun easily enough. He looked so much like her employer that it was obvious they were related. She and the older Mr. Farnsworth had been talking for about fifteen minutes when, in the course of their conversation, she mentioned she attended Vineyard Church. She recalled his words as if he had spoken them to her yesterday.

"Well then, Miss Pennington, since you attend The Vineyard Fellowship Church of Jesus Christ, tell me how it is you came to know that you have eternal life," he had said, an interested smile on his face.

"Excuse me?" she had asked, completely dumbfounded by his question.

"Since you go to church regularly and even teach Sunday school, have you come to the place in your life where you know for certain that, if you died today, you would go to heaven?" he had asked in return.

"Well," she had mumbled, taken aback by his question, "I think that it would be rather presumptuous to say 'yes,' but I. . .um. . .think so."

"It might surprise you to learn that such an unqualified 'yes' might not be at all presumptuous!" he had said kindly, seemingly unaware of her discomfort. "You know," he went on to say, "The Bible tells us that we can know for certain that we have eternal life. Did you know that?" He hadn't given her time to reply, but had continued on in his mellow, baritone voice.

"There was a time in my life when I not only didn't think I would go to heaven when I died, I knew I wouldn't. May I share with you how I came to know that I have eternal life—and how you can know it too?"

"I. . .guess so," she had replied, somewhat lamely.

Phillip had helped himself to a cup of coffee and offered

her one as well, which she refused. He had sat down leisurely at the table and motioned for her to do the same.

"First, let me ask you another question, if I may," he had said. "Suppose you were to die today and stand before God, and He were to say to you, 'Agatha, why should I let you into My heaven?' What would you say?"

Aggy remembered thinking this man rather impudent to be asking her, a Sunday school teacher and regular church attendee, such a question. He seemed genuinely curious, so she had thought intently before replying. She didn't think she had ever thought about such a thing before he had asked.

"I would tell Him I've always tried to do the right thing. That I obeyed the Ten Commandments and taught my students to do the same. I think that is what I would say to God."

"You know, Agatha," he had said, his dark eyes regarding her kindly, "In some ways I used to think like you. Granted," he had said with a chuckle, "I never taught Sunday school, but I thought I was better than average—maybe better than some Sunday school teachers!" He had paused for effect and she smiled with him. "Then I heard the greatest news I had ever heard in my life! I think you'll find it to be the greatest news you've ever heard, too. That is, that heaven is a gift! Isn't that great?" he had asked enthusiastically.

Agatha then heard and understood for the first time the gospel of Jesus Christ. Not the "gospel" as she had taught it for over thirty years, but the true gospel of God. With Phillip's clear, gentle presentation of the message of the Bible, that day

Agatha became a true follower of Jesus Christ. Her personal relationship with the Savior transformed her life and her teaching. She had once heard that life begins at forty. For her, life began at fifty. She often dubbed the first fifty years of her life as "B.C." and her life after being born again as "A.D." Unquestionably, Phillip had a part in her transformation as well. *That could not be denied,* she thought with fond remembrance.

Agatha Pennington became a bride that summer. She and Phillip, her new friend and mentor, wed within six months of their first meeting. Her days as a nanny were over and she became the wife of a very wealthy man. There were so many changes in her life that year! Phillip pampered her with gifts, attention, and trips to places she had never, ever considered seeing! He was not a handsome man, but he could dress up a deserved criticism with a smile and any recipient would accept it as a compliment. His winsome personality, genteel demeanor, and kind voice more than made up for his plain looks and halting gait. He still was the love of her life. Despite being confined to a bed now, he retained the humble dignity that had first drawn Aggy to him. Phillip did not begrudge God his degenerative disease. Rather, he praised Him for the conveniences of voice-activated computers, fax machines, and all the other types of communication technology that kept him connected to the outside world. Her Phillip was indeed a special man.

In the fall of 1975 she had met what was to be her final children's Sunday school class. She often thought of them as they looked when she first met them. Leah, with her piercingly pale blue eyes and strawberry-blond hair, was one of the most beautiful children Aggy had ever seen. Engaging, giggling Miriam had a large gap between her front teeth. Her lisping reading brought a smile of remembrance to Aggy's face. Joy and Dawn were cousins who asked more questions than the other five children together. Betsy was a tiny little thing who wore thick glasses. They made her brown eyes look too big for her cherubic face. The two boys, Sam and Conner, were always in competition or collusion to bring anarchy into their small classroom. Most of the time Aggy was able to keep them under control, but they had disrupted the class successfully not a few times during that fleeting year. Funny, Aggy couldn't remember the worst of their antics now. She remembered the happiest times.

She thought with some chagrin how guilty she had often felt that last year of teaching. Here she had been a Sunday school teacher for most of her life and had never really known Jesus at all! She had been zealous with this, her final class of students, to teach about Jesus and the Bible correctly. Her desire to make the children understand what it meant to be born again, to be a Christian, was often frustrated by her inability to present the gospel as clearly as Phillip had to her. He had helped her, but she was still awkward and less sure of her communication skills than she had ever been. She prayed for the salvation of each child faithfully. She and Phillip, with no children of their own, often took The Seven on outings or elaborate excursions. Through that memorable year, she and Phillip personally prayed with four of The Seven to receive Jesus Christ as Lord and Savior. Little Betsy had "prayed Jesus into her heart," as she said it, at the age of four. Joy had later become a Christian as a teenager. That left only Conner. When it was time for her last class of children to move up to their next Sunday school class, Conner, to Aggy's knowledge, had not prayed for salvation. When gently approached by Phillip or Aggy, he was not belligerent or defiant. He simply was indifferent; something else would always catch his attention.

Aggy had maintained friendships with the children as much as possible in the ensuing years, but her and Phillip's frequent trips abroad, and the nature of children themselves to develop other friendships, meant she often observed them from a distance. The families of Miriam, Conner, and Joy had moved out of town. Sam's family joined another church when he was not quite a teenager, and Dawn too now attended another church. Only Leah and Betsy remained at Vineyard. Betsy was married with a young child of her own now. She always greeted Aggy and once or twice a year stopped by to visit Phillip. However, it was Leah who remained their special "daughter."

There was nobody like their dear Leah. She had grown from a beautiful child into a winsome, engaging woman. She was a delight to Aggy and Phillip. She came by their house every week or so with her merry eyes and unrestrained chatter. Aggy thought she must be the world's sole twenty-seven-year-old tomboy. Just last week she had pulled into the driveway, her tires bringing the car to a shrieking halt. Phillip had scarcely looked up from the newspaper.

"That'll be our Leah," he said.

"Hey! Anybody home in this drafty old castle?" Leah yelled up the staircase, already bounding up the stairs by twos.

"You know I'm not at the tennis court, young lady," Phillip called back sternly, but he winked at Aggy.

Leah came into the room, her curly hair peaking out from under her ball cap and her soccer uniform bearing the marks of a hard-fought match.

"Hello, dear," Aggy said, giving her a kiss on the cheek. She noted with a smile Leah's rosy cheeks and flashing eyes. Her pale blue eyes always seemed lighter, almost other-worldly after she had been out in the sun. *She was often their sunshine,* Aggy concluded mentally. "Would you like some juice or soda pop?"

"Nah. I'm fine. We won and went out for a burger and something to drink after the game. How ya doin', Pops?" she asked Phillip, planting a kiss on his forehead.

"Just fine, Leah. And this house is not drafty," he corrected with a smile.

"This castle is drafty. Why don't you sell it and buy one of those new condos out on the lake?" She plopped into the chair nearest Phillip and reached for a mint from the nightstand.

"This is home. We like our yard," Phillip returned, well familiar with the direction their conversation was going.

"The grounds," Leah corrected, suddenly assuming a British accent and lifting her perky nose in the air, "require you to keep on three gardeners." She dropped her playacting at the end of that one sentence and pointed a finger at Phillip. "We all know neither of you uses the pool or tennis court anymore. You don't entertain that much, and you could make some really serious money if you'd break down and sell this expanse. The developers around here drool over this place like vultures over fresh roadkill. You could sell it in a minute and buy a conservative, one-story abode. No need for an elevator and no steps for Aggy to have to navigate."

"I get around just fine, thank you," Aggy put in. "And we've never had a minute's trouble with the elevator."

"Well, I worry about you sometimes in this big old castle with those marble floors," Leah remarked, barely contrite.

"We plan to leave this 'big old castle' to you when we're gone, young lady. So you had better speak of it with more respect," Phillip said, doing some of his own finger-pointing. "Then you can deal with the 'vultures,' as you call them."

"Don't you dare leave this rambling old palace to me!" Leah exclaimed. "The taxes would put me in the poorhouse within six months!"

"Well, then, I guess you will have to deal with the vultures," he retorted, smugly confident that he had won this one tête-à-tête. Leah was not to be outdone so easily.

"Keep it up, Pops, and I'll turn you into a practice goalie for my soccer team—bed and all!"

That was how their visits often went. Leah's gaiety and banter would leave Agatha and Phillip chuckling for hours after she left. They kept waiting for her to bring a "someone special" over, but it never happened. She simply didn't have "time for men—or a man," as she phrased it. In spite of her attractiveness, she rarely dated. She seemed content with her job, small apartment, and ongoing assortment of sports: soccer, softball, volleyball, and more. Her parents had both died in an automobile accident when Leah was in college and Aggy and Phillip had readily stepped in as "parents" for her. However, she had always refused any financial assistance from them. When she graduated from college, Phillip had given her his 1963 convertible sports car. She tried to refuse the lavish gift, but Phillip would not hear of it.

"Besides," Aggy had quipped, "if it sits in our garage one more year, I might have to start driving it around again! And we all know what a disaster that might turn out to be!"

Leah's tearful, boisterous gratefulness for the generous gift had pleased Phillip immensely. It had been his idea and he had laughingly confided to Aggy that he couldn't stand the thought of people driving by and wondering why a beat-up, ugly, white-and-rust compact car always sat on the circular drive in front of the Farnsworth Estate.

"I don't think I'm being a snob," he had said, "but you must admit Leah's pile of rusted metal on wheels is something of an eyesore. And Marvin claims the exhaust from her engine is hard on the more fragile shrubs. He worries about those silly bushes, you know."

So they had given the car to Leah. They didn't have to concern themselves with how her car looked in the drive now, but the squealing tires and blaring radio on the warm days when the convertible top was off made them wonder if they would have been wiser to leave well enough alone. They always heard Leah arrive long before they saw her. She had been much less intrusive upon her arrival in her old compact.

"Hello, Miss Aggy."

Aggy looked up from her mental wanderings to a tall young man with curly black hair and a closely trimmed beard and mustache. She would have been captured by his handsome face if she wasn't stupefied by his size. He towered over her and the span of his shoulders made two of hers.

"Miss Aggy?" he repeated. "It's me. Conner."

"Conner?" Aggy gasped in delighted surprise. "Let me look at you!" She stood and clasped both his huge hands in her small, delicate ones. She had to look up, up, up at him and her eyes sparkled with glee.

"Dear, dear Conner. Wait until Phillip sees you! Here, sit beside me where I can see your face." Conner did as he was told, his smile one of indulgent submission.

"I'm so glad Sam was able to locate you! I was afraid you had disappeared! Tell me where you've been and what you've been doing for the last twenty years," she said. Aggy held onto one of his hands, still marveling that this imposing giant was the mischievous Conner that had sat Sunday after Sunday in her class of second-graders.

"No, first of all you tell me about you, Phillip, and Vineyard. This is quite a place!" He looked around them.

"You'll hear all about us once everyone is here. You first," she demanded.

"Aggy? Is that you, C. J.?" The two of them looked up at another young man, of much smaller stature than Conner, his hand reaching out to grasp Conner's.

"Sam!" they both said at once. Sam shook Conner's hand vigorously and bent down to kiss Aggy lightly on the cheek.

"Miss seeing you on the tube, C. J. I always enjoyed bragging to my wife that 'I knew you when. . . .' Miss Aggy, you are as stunning as ever!" he declared affably.

"And you are still the sweet-talker you were as a little boy, Samuel! Do you mean to tell me Conner was a television star?" Aggy asked. She had no idea Conner had been on television. She and Phillip rarely watched any television programs. Sam laughed.

"Don't tell me you and Phillip never watched football star C. J. Marino taking out quarterbacks and receivers like so many ducks in a row!" Aggy looked at Conner, who seemed embarrassed in a pleasant way. "This guy," Sam continued, his hand on one of Conner's massive shoulders, "was pro football with a capital 'P' up until a few years ago. Doesn't Phillip ever watch football? You haven't heard of C. J. Marino?" Sam's words came out in a running staccato.

"I'm embarrassed to say, 'no,' " Aggy replied. "But Conner's last name is Sturtt, as I recall."

"That's right, Miss Aggy. You wouldn't have known! My mom married after we moved from here and Tony legally adopted me. It's a good thing you had Sam track me down. You would have never located Conner Sturtt!" he said with a laugh.

The noise increased around them with the arrival of other people. As more members of their own reunited group arrived, their laughter and exclamations of surprise were a festive match for all the other greetings around them. The afternoon was a collage of renewed friendships and remembered accounts told over and over in snatches amid laughter and easy banter. The planned program briefly interrupted their socializing, but they all knew they would have more time in the evening to continue their reacquaintance. Leah had arranged to be with Phillip and assure everything at the Farnsworths' was ready for the weekend. With the exception of Betsy, the former 1975 second grade Sunday school of Vineyard Fellowship Church would be staying the weekend with Phillip and Aggy. Aggy wished all of The Seven could be there, but it wasn't possible. Dawn was overseas and Joy and her husband were in youth ministry out West.

After the light luncheon, the program began and Aggy's former class of children was seated around her. She would steal glances at each of them. She was awed by the wonderful things God had done in and through them. She thought she must know how a mother feels having her grown children gather around her for a family get-together. Aggy anticipated their time together at home—all of them. She and Phillip would keep them up all night to learn everything about them, if they had to! She was eager to get home and share "the children" with Phillip. After the program, each of them prepared to drive to the Farnsworth residence, where Betsy would later join them. Conner had come by taxi from the airport and rode home with Aggy.

"I simply cannot call you 'C. J.,' Conner," she said as they pulled out into traffic. "It just doesn't fit."

"That's fine, Miss Aggy. You call me whatever it is you want," he said warmly.

"Why don't you fill me in on the rest of your life, Conner. You don't play football now?"

"No. Bad knees made short work of an even shorter career. I started having trouble as early as college, but kept at it until surgery and medication could no longer get me through one quarter of play, let alone a whole game or season. Now I coach football at a small college outside of Atlanta, but I'm looking for a new position," he said. "Like I said in my letter, that's why I asked you and Phillip about staying a few extra days. I have an interview at the university for a defensive coaching position."

"We were so happy when you said you'd be here for a while. I'm glad you took Phillip's advice and didn't rent a car. We still have two and I obviously cannot drive both of them at once. What else, Conner? There's got to be more to your life than football," she baited, wanting to learn more about him.

"Well, let's see. . .I've developed a fascination with ultra-light aircraft, and I've been taking flying lessons. I have a cat named Edgar. I'm not married and not looking. I lead a men's Bible study at church. . . ."

"Bible? Have you become a Christian then, Conner?" Aggy asked, glancing at him with the hopeful question reflected on her face.

"Yes, Miss Aggy," he said gently. "How could I not with all the love and attention you and Phillip showered on me for as long as I was here in Ohio and at Vineyard? But I'll tell you more about it later so I don't have to tell it all to Phillip again. How is he? I thought he would be there this afternoon."

"He is good mentally and, of course, he is always in

good spirits. But he is confined to his bed now, Conner. Up until last year he was still able to get around in a wheelchair occasionally, but it's not possible now. A few hours a day he can be in a chair, but it is very painful for him. He really isn't able to get out at all—except in our own yard—when he needs the fresh air and sunshine more than the relative comfort of his bed. But we manage and have a visiting nurse service as needed. One of our gardeners is close to us and spends much of his time helping Phillip with his personal hygiene needs or things that I'm unable to do. We do fine. And Leah is there quite often to help as well."

"I vaguely remember Leah. How is she? What does she do now?" he asked.

"She's fine. She is still a chatterbox, however, so I'll let her tell you all about herself. Both she and Betsy have remained close to us through the years. Betsy has her own family now, however, so she is not able to keep tabs on us like Leah does. Leah really is the daughter we never had, Conner. She is a balm and delight for both of us with her happy chatter and outgoing disposition. Here we are!" she said, turning as the remote-controlled white iron gate opened before them.

"The old place looks as impressive as ever, Miss Aggy," Conner said as they pulled into the drive. "I was so intimidated the first time you brought all of us here. I went home and asked my mother if you and Phillip were richer than the president. My mom laughed and said, 'Much richer, son.' I was in awe of Phillip and this place! Still am, I think," he mused aloud.

"A house is just a house, Conner. It's who's inside it that

counts. And Who's inside those inside. Don't worry about your bags. We asked Jonathan to come out of retirement for the weekend and he'll tend to it. Max will see to the car."

The portly Max opened her door as Aggy stopped the car and Jonathan greeted Conner with some awe as he shook his hand and then went to get Conner's luggage from the trunk. Miriam and Sam pulled in behind them; Betsy had gone home to fix supper and put her daughter to bed. The laughter of the noisy foursome bounced around the ornate foyer as they remarked on how little the Farnsworth Estate had changed in the last twenty years.

"Who are all those noisy kids out there coming to tear up my house?" called Phillip from the adjoining sitting room. Aggy went to him with a pleased smile.

"How did you all manage to arrange this? It's wonderful!" Aggy said, looking around at the hospital bed and furnishings neatly arranged in their parlor.

"Leah, Jonathan, and Marvin pulled it off. Leah said we needed to make more use of that elevator and bought this fancy hospital bed so I can lie around someplace else in the house. Come here, my children, so I can see you!" he said, pleasure evident on his face. He lifted his arms in invitation.

Aggy laughed as Phillip made over each of them as she had. Leah had come into the room and squealed with delight as she hugged Miriam. She grabbed hold of both of Sam's hands. With her usual unrestrained enthusiasm, she began talking excitedly. Conner stood to his full height after embracing Phillip. He turned to Leah, whose excited chatter ceased immediately. Sam and Miriam had turned to greet and hug Phillip, so only Aggy saw and felt what transpired in those immediate seconds as Leah's eyes took in Conner. He smiled broadly at the striking woman before him. Leah, for the first time since Aggy had known her, was speechless. Conner regarded Leah with obvious interest. The air between them was electric with unspoken discovery. But Leah stood there openmouthed and wide-eyed. Aggy moved to her as quickly as she could, grasping her hand. She sensed that (fortunately) Conner had not succumbed to the same stupefying inertia that had suddenly enveloped Leah. Aggy propelled her towards Conner.

"You remember Conner, don't you, Leah?" Aggy intoned, knowing very well that Leah did remember Conner. More than likely not this Conner.

"Leah," Conner extended his hand. "You look wonderful. All grown up. It's nice to see you again."

Leah smiled in return, but it was a strained smile. She did not shake Conner's offered hand. Aggy doubted she even saw it. Leah dropped her wide-eyed gaze immediately from Conner's handsome face to some place on her shoe. She did not speak. She did not bombard him with a hundred questions at once. And she most certainly did not embrace him as she had Sam and Miriam. She simply stood there: her cheeks crimson, her long eyelashes hiding her pale blue eyes, and her front teeth biting down slightly on the edge of her lower lip.

Aggy had never seen Leah act like this! She saw Conner drop his hand; Aggy quickly tried to salvage a very uncomfortable moment. Leah's sudden, uncharacteristic, inarticulate paralysis temporarily left Aggy speechless herself. *Well, it must be Conner's imposing appearance,* she thought. It was disconcerting at first.

"Leah, sweetheart, did you know that our Conner is the same man as C. J. Marino, former linebacker for. . .um. . . ," Aggy couldn't recall which team.

"The Kings," Leah finished for her. "And formerly of the University of Wisconsin. No, I didn't. Not until today." Conner continued to smile at her, but Leah barely looked at him.

Well, Aggy thought, *at least she managed to get a few words out!*

"Have Jonathan call out for some pizza, Aggy! I'm famished!" Phillip called to her from his bed.

"Hungry? We just stuffed ourselves over at the church!" Sam laughed.

"You stuffed yourself, Sam Watson! I was too busy talking to eat anything! How about you, Conner?" Miriam asked from where she sat next to Phillip.

"I can always eat," he said to Miriam, but his eyes didn't leave Leah, who remained uncharacteristically quiet.

"Well, it will take a while," Aggy said. "Meanwhile you all decide what kind you would like and I'll have Jonathan get us something to drink."

They all settled comfortably around Phillip's bed and took up where they had left off in the course of their conversation at church. Aggy noted that Leah contributed little, except when asked, and she seemed to struggle with talking even then. Phillip caught Aggy's eye and winked. So, he had not missed what was happening either. Aggy contented herself with Leah's sudden diffidence and joined in the conversation with a settled pleasure. This might turn out to be an even better weekend than she had imagined!

After eating their pizza, and once Betsy arrived, the elderly couple and their young guests grew more serious and intense in their conversations. It was Phillip who kept the discussion coming back to important things. Aggy did too, but Phillip was the one who could keep the topic on track.

"All right now," he said, clapping his hands together once for emphasis. "We need to hear the best of the best. Tell us the high point of your last, let's say, five years. I'll even start to give you all time to think about it. Aggy, if you'd go second, that would give them an extra hour or two more to think of something to say."

She shook her finger at him with good-natured rebuke. "Watch it, old man, or I'll have this gorilla here toss you out!" She patted Conner's arm.

"Okay. Here we go," Phillip paused before continuing. "Probably the highest point in the last five years has been being confined to this old bed. While Agatha is out and about (when I'm able to convince her that I'll be fine for a few hours on my own), I have been able to know God better. I pore over His word and then tear commentaries apart rather than vice versa."

"That doesn't surprise any of us one bit, Phillip," Sam said, his grin wide.

"I have learned what Paul talked about—being content

in all circumstances. You all know we don't lack for things or money, but good health and mobility are in short supply at the Farnsworth house. So every day Aggy and I have, I enjoy. Leah has been a blessing to us too. I can't pick out one particular event—just the growing confidence that the Lord is in control and I don't have to worry even if only about 50 percent of me is in working order." He rubbed his thin hands together. "Okay, dear one, your turn," he said to Aggy.

"Today is the day for me. I can't tell you what a delight it is to see you all again. All of you have been special to us and I have so looked forward to this day. You know," she continued, "you were the first and last Sunday school class I taught as a Christian. Sometimes that has caused me grief of spirit, but I just return to Romans 8, where God assures us that we are under no condemnation in Christ."

Phillip smiled at his wife. How often they had come back to that passage when Aggy had her bouts of depression! Only in recent years had she been able to leave the unsaid, undone things of the past in the past. It had brought healing for her and relief to him.

"I don't know which of you arranged it," Aggy continued, "but having a telephone call from Joy this morning and E-mail from Dawn certainly rounded out this celebration for me. It reminds me again that God is good and that He is good all the time."

Sam told of the birth of his triplets who were now four years old. He had brought a huge album full of pictures of his wife and three sons. They laughed with him over the boys' antics and teased him about not bringing the whole family with him. He spoke tenderly of how his own fatherhood had taught him much of the Fatherhood of God. Aggy squeezed Phillip's hand as he talked. "Their" Sam was a man of depth and diversity.

Miriam had recently gotten engaged and talked about the plans she and her soon-to-be husband were making for their life together. She was a gifted vocalist trying to break into the recording industry and her fiancé was her manager. She talked of the frustrations of being an "unknown" and trying to make her way into a professional career in music.

"I remember you two guys," she said, pointing at Sam and Conner, "teasing me unmercifully about my lisp! Well, my teeth came in and I can talk—and sing, thank you— without lisping now!" They laughed as a group at the memory and Miriam's good-natured rebuke.

Betsy told of her struggle with infertility in the first years of her marriage and the joy of finally conceiving Faith. She promised to bring her daughter over the next day, stating that Faith was definitely a "morning person" and they would not have found her very much fun this evening.

Leah began haltingly, but in a short time was more like herself. She talked with her usual exuberance about her coaching of a girls' soccer team. She spoke tenderly of Aggy and Phillip's care and support of her through the loss of her parents. As she talked, Aggy noticed that Leah seldom looked at Conner. She also noted that Conner's eyes were riveted on Leah.

The gathered group indulged in more light conversation before Phillip finally demanded to hear Conner's tale.

Conner briefly told of his short career in professional football, the blow it was to him when he could no longer play, but the help he received from a fellow team member.

"My whole life had been football," he said, refusing more offered pizza from Aggy. "With Cary's help I not only was able to let go of the one passion of my life, I was able to pursue another. Cary introduced me to Jesus. It was funny how so much of what he said echoed things you had said to me when I was a child, Phillip. Of course, it was now on an adult level, but I recalled your admonitions and your teaching too, Aggy. After I prayed to receive Christ as my Lord and Savior, I often thought back to my last Sunday school year here. Until Cary came along, I hadn't been to a church since Mom and I had moved. Cary still remains my mentor, although we maintain our friendship by phone and letter. But that certainly was one of the high points of my life in the last five years. And coming here today too. I really appreciate the invitation, you two," he said to Aggy and Phillip. The others in the room nodded or verbalized their agreement with Conner's statement.

"Well, the pleasure is certainly all ours, children," Phillip said.

The rest of the evening continued on in a relaxed atmosphere of conversation and laughter. An occasional tear would come with a remembrance or a sharing of a difficult time in the life of one of them, but Sam's good humor would restore levity to the overall tone of their discussion. By shortly after midnight, Aggy had everyone assigned to his or her own room. She came in to give her husband a kiss good night and have their final time of prayer together before retiring.

"What are you grinning about, my dear wife?" Phillip asked as she settled in the chair closest to his bed.

"Who, me?" she asked with feigned innocence. She removed her eyeglasses and set them on the nightstand. "I would love to be a little mouse right now. I sent Leah down to make sure the alarm system was set."

"I'm sure Jonathan saw to that," Phillip stated.

"Probably. But it doesn't hurt to have someone double-check. I also sent Conner down to make sure the lights were off in the parlor."

"Even though you can check and control that from up here."

"Even though I can check and control that from up here. Now, let's get to praying, my husband," she said, patting his hand affectionately.

"We had better pray about your sudden lapse into matchmaking under false pretenses," Phillip said, a small smile playing about his mouth.

"Yes," Aggy said, "we can pray about that, too."

"Oh! You startled me!" Leah exclaimed, finding Conner standing a few feet behind her as she turned from the panel by the front door.

"Sorry, Leah. I didn't mean to," Conner apologized. "Aggy sent me down to check the lights in the parlor." He turned to go to the parlor and Leah followed him.

"But she can. . ." Leah stopped midsentence.

"Can what?" he asked. He turned back to face her.

"Can. . .uh. . ." Leah realized she and Conner had been duped. She kept the knowledge to herself. "Oh, nothing. Say," she said, quickly changing the subject, "How is it your name is Marino now? Wasn't it Sturd or Sturtt or something when we were kids here?"

"Like I told Aggy," he said, sitting down in the recliner and propping up the footrest, "My stepdad legally adopted me when he and Mom got married. My biological dad never had anything to do with Mom or me, so it was fine by me and Tony has never treated me any different than he does his and Mom's other kids. I got three brothers and four sisters after Tony and Mom wed. He's just 'Dad' to me like he is to the rest of the gang, although they are all so much younger than me. Have a seat, Leah," he said, motioning for her to sit down. She sat.

The silence that ensued was disquieting for Leah. She couldn't believe she sat in the same room with C. J. Marino! *The* C. J. Marino! He was disarmingly handsome, power-fully built, and taller than anyone she had ever met. She had watched him play throughout his college career and had known of his signing-on with the Kings. She remembered ogling and giggling over him with her girlfriends in college. When a group would gather to watch a big game on televi-sion, they would choose the Most Valuable Player of the game. However, the girls' choice was never based on the player's abilities. Their male colleagues would groan, laugh, or agree, depending on the selected player's performance. It had been fun and was a fond memory for her. Yet she had never known C. J. Marino and Conner Sturtt were one and the same. Why would she have? Out of sight was out of mind! She had forgotten all about him (and others) in that long-ago Sunday school class. Phillip and Aggy were the ones to bring back those old memories when they had eagerly begun preparing for this weekend.

Conner seemed genuine and not at all self-obsessed. In fact, she decided he was too good to be true. She concluded he was probably engaged, or had already been married four times. Conner clasped his hands behind his head. His biceps stretched the sleeves of his shirt taut and Leah dropped her eyes to the floor. This guy was just too incredibly good-looking for his own good! She wanted to run from the room, yet she wanted to stay, too. She could not remember ever being so physically attracted to a man. Leah felt cold, but her hands were sweating. She wasn't all that sure she wouldn't just throw up.

"So, just how tall are you, anyway?" she asked. *Dumb, Leah,* she said to herself. *That was really dumb.*

She was relieved (somewhat) when Conner laughed. "Well, once you do start talking, you're certainly direct, Leah. I'm six-foot-seven and yes, I have a terrible time finding clothes that fit. Anything else?" he asked.

"I'm sorry. That was in poor taste," she said in reply.

"Nah—it's a natural question, I think. I've had it asked and answered it so often that I almost tell people how tall I am when we're introduced," he said, his smile easy.

"Was it fun being a professional athlete?" she asked, genuinely curious.

"I never really enjoyed the celebrity status that goes along with a successful sports career and towering above most people, but that's just the way it is. It had its kudos, but it had just as many negatives, to be honest. It's not so bad now that I'm out of the limelight."

He stopped briefly and regarded Leah with his blue eyes. Leah couldn't help but notice the way his black eyelashes made the color of his eyes seem all the more pronounced. She hoped she wasn't being obvious in her study of him. She concentrated briefly on the opal she always wore on her right ring finger.

"But let's talk about you, Leah," he said. "What do you do for a living? Are you interested in sports other than soccer and volleyball? Do you have any brothers or sisters?"

"I work for a local law firm. I participate in almost every sport available to women in this city. I have an older brother and sister who live in Denver and San Diego," she replied. She tried to assume a posture of nonchalance, but she was having trouble thinking and talking. She did not remember ever feeling like this around a man. At least, not in recent history. She felt stupid, intimidated, and awkward.

"Do you run?" he asked.

"Three or four mornings a week," she replied.

"How about running with me in the morning before church?"

"Well, I run pretty early," she said, looking for a reason not to see Conner when she looked her worst.

"I can do early," he said, his smile flustering her more.

"I'm not a fast runner."

"Me neither."

"I only do a 5K," she said, trying to remember if that was the distance she usually ran.

"I can manage a slow 5K," Conner said, reaching down and releasing the footrest on the chair. He came to sit next to her.

Leah tried to remain calm, but she felt her heart racing and her face coloring. *Don't gasp. Don't drool. Don't throw up,* she kept repeating to herself. *Don't say anything else stupid.* Her heart was in overdrive; her brain was stalled.

"What about your bad knees?" Her voice sounded tight to her own ears. *Brilliant, Leah. Call the man a liar to his face.* Her mouth was dry. That was good. Maybe she wouldn't throw up.

"I can do limited running. Is it a date?" he asked lightly.

"Uh. . .sure. I'll need to go home for my running clothes."

"Great. I'll meet you here at six sharp." He stood and stretched. "Guess I'll turn in for the night. See you in the morning," he said cordially. He touched her lightly on the shoulder and left the room.

Leah closed her eyes and placed her hand where Conner had touched her to make sure it hadn't ignited or melted. His cologne still lingered in the air. She wrapped her other arm around herself. If this was love, she wasn't sure she liked it. "God, help me get my head back on straight," she whispered. She sat there for a long time before going to bed.

"Ready to go?" Conner asked, rising from the chair the next morning.

"Yes." She might as well have left her hot pepper spray at home. No worries when running alongside this man! Conner was dressed in a tank top and running shorts. Leah thought he looked like he'd been chiseled out of granite. Even though she had gotten up early to put on some makeup and try to make her hair passable, she knew she hardly resembled anything remotely statuesque. Leah decided there was no way Conner could not look good. She noted the knee brace on his right leg and scars around his left knee.

"Look like an old warhorse, don't I?" he said, laughing. They quietly walked out the front door after Leah reset the alarm.

" 'War horse' wasn't the first word that came to my mind," she said honestly.

"Wow! This is some car!" Conner exclaimed. "You one of the lawyers at the law firm?"

"Hardly. This was a gift from Phillip and Aggy. Don't get too excited. You might have to ride with your knees in your face. Or, we could strap you to the trunk," she quipped. "That would certainly create a stir—even early on a Sunday morning!"

"It certainly would, but I don't do trunks. Well, driver, I'm glad you left the convertible top at home." He groaned as he maneuvered himself into the seat next to Leah. "I may be half the man I was by the time we get to your place," he said with a final grunt.

"We'll change cars. My compact isn't much bigger, but you can't run if you're in the shape of a pretzel by the time we get to the park!" she laughed.

Leah dropped Conner off at Aggy and Phillip's after their short run. Even on her return trip to her duplex she could recall little of their conversation. Mostly they had talked about the Farnsworths, Conner asking Leah questions about his friends of years past. She went home to shower and change, careful to pick out something feminine, but discreet. Everyone was enjoying breakfast when she returned. Conner insisted on staying home with Phillip. Leah tried not to show her disappointment that Conner would not be going to church with them.

Once more Aggy sat with most of her final Sunday school class seated around her. She again reflected on the pure pleasure of having each of "her" children beside her. She gave Miriam's hand a fond squeeze and relished Sam's arm draped protectively across the pew behind her. She patted Leah's knee and received a warm smile in return.

"Disappointed that Conner stayed with Phillip?" she asked.

"Why would I be disappointed?" Leah asked in return. Aggy simply smiled at her and let the subject drop.

Leah tried to get her mind off Conner Marino and onto the service. She wished she had stayed with Phillip. She needed his serenity. Phillip had a way of always keeping things in perspective. Leah felt like she needed some perspective. She couldn't stop thinking about Conner.

"Are you all right, dear?" Aggy asked quietly. "You seem distracted."

If you only knew! Leah thought. But she smiled back at Aggy. "I'm fine, Aggy," she whispered.

"We'll talk later," Aggy said, and turned her attention to the pastor.

"Our text for today is taken from Matthew 14, starting at verse 15," he announced. "It's a familiar portion of scripture to many of you, but I want to draw some parallels for us today as we sit here in our new facility. . . ."

After the service, the busy weekend that had begun on Saturday continued at the Farnsworth Estate. In addition to their out-of-town guests, Aggy and Phillip had invited other close friends of many years and the parents of The Seven who were still in the area. The present pastoral staff, the past pastors and their wives were also included in the large gathering. Phillip was able to be up in his wheelchair for a few hours and the "drafty old castle" rang with talk, laughter, and the noise of children. It was an exhausting day for Phillip, but he and Aggy agreed it was worth the extra medication he would need in the evening. When the last guest had left and some tearful farewells had been spoken, Leah, Conner, and the Farnsworths gathered in Phillip's room.

"My, that was a great time!" Phillip remarked.

"Yes, but I think you overdid it, Pops," Leah said, standing to go and sit beside him. She raised his hand to her lips for a kiss and then continued to hold his hand with both of hers.

"Nonsense," he said abruptly, but Aggy agreed with Leah.

"Dear, would you show Conner where the keys are for the car and how to get around to the garage in case he's forgotten? Marvin and I will see to Phillip. Come, my love," she said to her husband, "you did overdo it today. Let's get you settled in for the night before you get your second wind and wear us both out!"

Leah gave Phillip her customary kiss on the forehead. She hugged Aggy and said her good nights to both of them, glad for the additional help they had hired to return the house to order.

"I'll see you two in the morning," Conner said, following Leah out the door.

The two of them descended the staircase. In spite of her distraction when alone with Conner, Leah was concerned about Phillip.

"You're worried about Phillip," Conner stated without preamble.

"A little. He hides it well, but he has a lot of pain when and after he's up in his wheelchair for that long. Aggy and Marvin will take care of him, but he'll probably not be able to even sit up at all tomorrow," she answered.

She led Conner down the hallway past the former servants' quarters and then to the servants' entrance which now served as a repository for additional keys, cleaning supplies, and other items of a practical nature.

"Okay," Leah said, opening a locked compartment inside an inconspicuous cabinet. "Here's a house key, a key for the car, an opener for the gate, and an opener for the garage." She placed each item in Conner's hand, noting that she would have never been able to hold all those things in one of her hands.

"Why do I need all these? Aren't there openers in Aggy's car?" he asked.

"Yes, but she wants you to take the black one. She never rides in it. Says it makes her feel like she's in a hearse."

Leah shut the safe door, spun the combination lock, and closed the cabinet. She turned, but Conner stood in front of her, his huge frame filling the doorway. There was no way she could get around him. She knew she couldn't go through him. She ventured making eye contact with him only to find him looking intently at her.

"Do you. . .know how to get to the garage from here?" she asked weakly. She wasn't sure she could remember at the moment.

"Leah," he said, taking her hand, "let's go out by the pool and have a talk. We were both so busy talking to everyone else today. And we couldn't really talk much this morning. You're one of the three people I've wanted to talk to the most and haven't been able to."

His touch was electrifying. *He wants me to talk?* she asked herself. *I'm having trouble just breathing!* It appeared Conner didn't notice. He pulled her from the confines of the small room.

"Is that old swing still there?" he asked. He set the keys and remote devices on a settee near the west entrance. He continued his hold on Leah's hand and led her outside. Leah didn't answer his question; she was thinking of what she would talk about with this man who set her heart to beating so wildly.

The fall evening was unseasonably warm and Leah was

glad she had changed earlier into a comfortable denim jumper and T-shirt. Conner pulled her gently to sit beside him on the oak swing they had swung on as children. To her relief—and simultaneous, slight disappointment—Conner released Leah's hand. He sat at the far end of the swing and casually began rocking back and forth.

Leah looked at him, the yard lights outlining his angular face. His beard was closely cut and did little to soften the hard angle of his jaw. But there was nothing hard in his eyes or the line of his mouth. Leah folded her hands together in her lap and took a deep breath to try and quell the butterflies that had once again taken up residence in her stomach.

"I want you to tell me more about you."

"Well," she laughed uneasily, "there really isn't much else to tell, Conner. What there is to me you've pretty much learned in the last two days."

"No, I haven't. For starters, are you seeing anyone?" he asked.

"No," she answered tersely. "Why? Are you?" There. The question she'd been wanting to ask was out.

"No. I haven't been for a long time," he answered, running his hand up the chain of the swing.

"Been married?" *Might as well get all the dirt,* she decided.

"No, but. . ."

Here it comes, she thought.

Conner turned to face her and moved towards her, slipping one of his massive arms behind her. Leah wasn't sure, but she thought she might faint for the first time in her life. Or melt into a quivering puddle of gelatin for the first time in her life. Her heart was pounding and she could scarcely breathe.

"This place hasn't changed much," he said in an abrupt change of subject. He looked wistfully across the water to the array of shrubs and plants that surrounded the pool deck. Few flowers were in bloom at this time of year. Leah waited for him to continue. "There's such a tranquility about this place. I think I sensed it even as a kid. It's like time slows down or stops once you come in the gate." He paused again. "Phillip tells me you are here several times a week."

"It's like home to me. He and Aggy are the closest thing I have to family here in town. And you're right about the tranquility. Some weeks at work force me to seek the refuge of this place. Phillip and Aggy are so close to Jesus that I have a greater sense of the presence of God here rather than at church sometimes. You know," she said, her thoughts momentarily focused on Aggy and Phillip, "they are a lifeline for me. They have nurtured me in the Word of God and loved me so that I can't imagine my life without them."

She smiled, more to herself than at Conner, remembering her thoughts of the morning. "Even this morning I was thinking how much I needed Phillip's serenity," she mused.

"Why?" Conner asked.

His one-word question brought Leah out of her reverie. "Why?" she repeated.

"I asked first," he said, a teasing glint in his eye.

"Why," she repeated flatly. She looked at Conner and could not think of a single additional word. She didn't need to. He gently pulled her into the circle of his embrace. Conner lifted her face to his and, in a breathless moment, kissed her tenderly. Leah kept her eyes closed, relishing the thrill that swept through her. Conner kissed her again, his own passion ignited by the willing submission he sensed in Leah. He released her and stood, walking to one of the portico's ornate columns.

Leah wasn't sure why Conner walked away so brusquely. For her part, she wasn't sure she would be able to stand at the moment, let alone walk. She placed her fingertips to her lips, still relishing the touch of his lips on hers. Conner stood, silently looking at the moonlit pool. She wanted to go to him and have him hold her again, but she stayed seated. She cleared her throat and nervously made an attempt at some light humor.

"What is it?" she asked. "Do I need a breath mint?"

He turned his gaze to her and gave her a small smile. "Not that I noticed, Lee," he said.

"Lee. . ." she murmured. "My dad was the only person who ever called me that."

"Is that bad? Would you rather I didn't? It just came out," he said, his words hinting at an apology.

"No, no. It's rather nice, actually," she answered. A few seconds of silence ensued.

"I think we should go in now. I want to be my sharpest for the interview tomorrow and I know you have to work," he said. He continued to gaze at the pool and surrounding yard. "This is smaller than I remember it, but more beautiful— especially at night." He turned back to Leah and held out his hand to her. "How about lunch tomorrow?"

"Where? What time?" Leah stood on shaky legs. Conner took her hand and she mutely walked beside him back into the house.

"You tell me. I don't know my way around town anymore and you know all the restaurants."

"Will you be coming from here or the university?" she asked.

"I assume the school. You give me directions and I'll pick you up in front of your office."

Leah wrote down the directions for him. He walked her to her car after she gathered her things.

"I'll see you at lunch, Leah," he said, opening the car door for her. He did not kiss her again. He gently touched his hand to her face and then stood back as Leah left. Through her rear window, Leah saw him wave. She drove home in a distracted state. She had to wait over twelve hours before seeing Conner again. She couldn't believe how much one person had changed her focus in two days. She needed to talk with Aggy and Phillip.

Her lunch with Conner the next day was enjoyable, but brief. He had to return to the university to meet with members of the present coaching staff and Leah had to return to work. Leah felt small next to Conner. He was even more imposing in his pinstriped navy suit than he had been in his running attire. She did not miss the turned heads and interested looks of other women while they ate or after they exited the restaurant and stood talking for a few more minutes before going their separate ways. Leah felt loving a man such as Conner, if she did love him or grow to love him, might be a constant struggle with jealousy or suspicion. Perhaps Conner was right: imposing size and stunning good looks had their drawbacks. The combination not only had drawbacks for him, but also for the woman who might be his wife. Leah shook her head to dismiss the thought. Her heart was again muddling her common sense. After their brief lunch, concentration at work the rest of the day was difficult, at best.

That evening, Conner and Leah relaxed with Aggy and Phillip in Phillip's room. Conner's interview had gone well, but he was still going to investigate job possibilities at another smaller college fifty miles from the city.

"Now that I'm back in Ohio again I've decided I'd like to return here," Conner said.

"You might change your mind once the snow starts, but you know you have a refuge here anytime you need it, son," Phillip said, trying to make himself more comfortable.

" 'Son,' " Conner repeated. "It's funny you should use that word just now, Phillip, because I have something to ask you." He leaned forward, bringing his hands together and regarding Phillip intensely with his blue eyes. Both Aggy and Leah looked at Conner questioningly.

"I have more reasons to return to Ohio than a possible job. There's the two of you, my family just a couple hours away, and now, Leah." He turned his eyes on Leah and she felt herself blush.

"Are you interested in our Leah, Conner?" Aggy asked with a poorly concealed twinkle in her eye. She stopped her knitting momentarily.

"I'm past 'interested,' " he said with no hint of a smile. He turned again to face Phillip. "Since you are the closest thing to a father that Leah has, I'm asking your permission to court her."

Leah was stunned. Was this guy for real? "Court her?" Where did he get off asking such a stupid question? She was humiliated and appalled that Conner would say such a thing to Phillip—especially before saying anything to her! Besides, she was hardly a fourteen-year-old girl!

Beside her, Aggy let out an excited giggle and threw her hands up.

"Court our Leah? What a wonderful idea!" Aggy exclaimed.

"Excuse me," Leah said abruptly, trying not to sound too harsh, "but Conner has not discussed this with me."

"Let the man finish what he has to say, my dears," said Phillip from his bed. "Sit back down, Leah. Aggy, you hold your enthusiasm in check." He turned his attention back to Conner. "Why do you think it's necessary to ask my permission, Conner?" Phillip asked quietly.

Leah sat back down, but she was angry with Conner for his presumption and a little angry with Aggy for encouraging Conner with her response. She only sat because Phillip ordered her to do so. He had never "ordered" her to do anything in her life.

"Why, I repeat, did you come to me first, Conner? Leah is, after all, a grown woman and a mature Christian. She's very capable of making her own decisions—especially in regard to matters of the heart." Phillip met Conner's eyes with his own and seemed not the least surprised or rattled by Conner's question.

"Because neither of us is thinking straight right now. I don't want to appear audacious, but I think it's safe to say Leah is as attracted to me as I am to her. I want to know up front that, if this is headed where I think it is, I have your approval. It's important to me, but I know it's far more important to Leah. The passion of the moment may cause us to lose sight of the bigger picture. Whether I get this job at the university is incidental. Football being football, even getting this position doesn't mean I'd stay in this area. If I court Leah, which I would with your permission, it may be that someday she would have to leave here. . .that she would have to leave you. I will court her with a specific goal in mind. I don't do this lightly."

Leah couldn't believe what she was hearing. How dare he speak for her in this regard! Her face and neck were hot from the embarrassment and anger growing inside her. And, of course, she could never, ever leave Aggy and Phillip!

"What of you, Leah?" Phillip asked quietly. "Would you receive Conner's attentions? Are you as interested in him as he is in you?"

"Well, I. . ." *How could you put me in this position, Conner?* Leah thought angrily. But one look at him and her indignation vanished. "Yes, Pops," was all she said. She'd been acting like a smitten, silly, speechless schoolgirl all weekend. She was sure it was obvious to Phillip and Aggy—and Conner, too. She had never, ever been so attracted to a man before in her life. She wished it were not so, but it was. C. J. Marino had stepped out of college daydreams into her present reality. Now her reality was more dreamlike than anything she could have ever imagined. But to leave Phillip and Aggy? That she would never do! She couldn't!

"I have never 'courted' a woman before," Conner went on. "To be quite honest, I've hardly dated since becoming a Christian. Before I was born again, the idea of courtship never entered my head. A lot about me changed with my new birth. This was something I determined to do the next time I met a woman I was seriously interested in. This may be a whirlwind romance that ends up at the altar in less time than it took me to prepare this speech, but I wanted everything out front at the start. I would not willingly take Leah away from you, but it may happen. I owe the two of you too much to do that without your consent."

Everyone was silent with his own thoughts. Conner walked to stand behind Leah and rest his hands on her shoulders. She closed her eyes. How would she ever choose, if she had to?

"Of course," Conner continued, "I may be way out of line here altogether. I've not talked about this with Leah herself. And too, nothing may come of this at all. But I don't think that will be the case and I don't intend to start something I can't finish. It won't start, however, without your permission. That much I've determined."

"Well, my boy, you know you have the blessing of us both. This matter of Leah eventually leaving, should that happen, is incidental," Phillip replied. "It would be difficult

for us, but it is the Lord who sustains us and not our dear
Leah. Our time for good-byes will come sooner or later, one
way or another. That is part of life. So, if our tomboy will
permit you, we gladly give our permission for this courtship.
And, quite frankly, I like the idea of it!"

"Now that we have that settled, why don't the two of
you run out and get us some frozen yogurt or ice cream?"
asked Aggy lightly.

"Good idea," said Conner, coming around Leah and
taking her hand to pull her to her feet.

"Could I have a word with Leah first, son?" asked
Phillip. Conner gave Leah's hand a squeeze and left the room,
closing the door behind him. Leah came to Phillip's side in
something akin to a fog over the conversation of the last several minutes. Phillip took both her hands in his as she sat
beside him.

"Wait on God, my child. Leaving your childhood behind has been much longer in coming for you than it is for
most. Do not think loving Conner will mean leaving us in
the most important sense of the word. This may simply be a
new chapter in your life's book."

"Just like it was when Phillip met and married this old
spinster," Aggy added, bending down to kiss Leah's cheek.
"Now go to this man who may well fill the pages of the rest
of your life. Trust God, dear one. Learn as much about
Conner as you can and do not neglect to pray."

Leah left the room and found Conner waiting by the
staircase. Her heart was too full and her mind a tangle of
thoughts and emotions. She stepped timidly, but willingly,

into the circle of his embrace. They would talk, or argue, later.

"The weekend was, I should say, quite a success," Aggy murmured, sitting on the bed close to her husband.

"It was. Hopefully, we will have our Seven and then some back again for a wedding. I had gathered from my time with Conner yesterday that he was quite taken with our Leah. Leah's complete captivation with young Conner would be obvious to a blind man!" he said with a snicker.

"You think they're right for each other?" she asked.

"Were we?" he retorted, patting her hand fondly. "As I recall, we had our own 'whirlwind romance'! If they are not, we'll pray that God will make that clear to them early on. But I have a good feeling about this budding romance. I suspect Conner is coming into this relationship with some pre-Christian baggage, but our Leah will be just the one to help him sort through it all. And I like the sound of this friendship Conner has with that fellow, Cary. He sounds like a good mentor for our son in the faith." He picked up his eyeglasses from the bedside table. "Get my Bible, Agatha. I think it may be some time before we get that yogurt tonight!"

CHAPTER 6

The Gift

Essie's feet were out of her shoes and her earrings off before she shut the door behind her. She flipped on the light switch and deposited her purse and books on the kitchen table. Rinsing out a glass and filling it with water as cold as her faucet could produce on such short notice, her long, slow drink ended in a deep sigh. Today was the first day that spring really did seem to be arriving at last. She began opening the day's mail as she sank wearily into her favorite chair next to Franklin. He stretched out one paw in protest of the now-crowded conditions, but his yawn declared the territory not worth a fight. His big orange eyes were closed almost before they had opened.

"You know, Franklin, the 'Sabbath was made for man,' but," she gently rubbed his graying ears, "Wednesdays could not have been made for man, woman, nor beast." Her eyelids had begun the same weary descent as her cat's had when the telephone roused Essie back to full wakefulness.

"Hi, Mom. Did you just get home?" asked her oldest

daughter on the other end of the line. Essie could visualize Janell expertly balancing the receiver on her shoulder as she noisily loaded, or unloaded, her dishwasher. "Yes, Jan. Franklin and I were having our final discussion of the day before I turn in for the night. What's on your mind?" Essie suppressed a yawn and wiggled her toes.

"Tad will be in Chicago the rest of the week on business and so the girls thought the four of us could do something special for your birthday."

"Just what do those two have in mind this time?" asked Essie. Her teenaged granddaughters had a penchant for mischief when it came to birthdays. She could hear giggles in the background and a "Don't you give it away, Mom!" shouted over the din of banging pans and dishware.

"That is our little secret, Granny. You'll have to join us for a trip to the mall for your unique gift." Essie could detect a smirk on Jan's face by the tone of her voice. "I think you'll be tickled with the girls' originality on this one! They're just like Dad was when it comes to surprise gifts. So, should we meet at the mall about five tomorrow?"

"Sounds good, honey. The girls don't have school Friday, do they? Teachers' conference or something going on?" Essie asked.

"Right. Why?"

"I was wondering if they could stay overnight and help me start sorting through all the junk around here for our upcoming garage sale." Essie heard Janell repeat her request to the girls.

"They would love to, Mom. We'll see you at five o'clock

tomorrow. Be ready for a new you come Thursday! We love you." Their exchanged good-byes freed Essie to get up again and throw the balance of the mail into the wastebasket. She was just reaching for the light when the telephone rang again.

"I'm going to get one of those answering machines," she mumbled to herself. "Now, who is it at this time of night?" she asked the immovable pile of purring fur on her chair. As she greeted her caller she noted with some chagrin that she was feeling more awake as the minutes passed.

"Hello, Esther. I'm sorry to be calling so late. This is Will. Did I waken you?"

"No, you didn't. How are you, Will? Did you have a good fishing trip?" Essie sat back down next to the cat, who evidently decided he might as well get something to eat until all the activity was over. Essie recalled Will telling her he would be out of town for a week or so. She and Will Davidson had had numerous contacts during the three years she had been the bookkeeper for a group of family practice physicians. Will's accounting firm down the hall from their office had handled their accounts for years, so it followed she had come to know him through their businesses.

"Great trip. Great fishing. My brother's youngest boy, Robbie, is a fisherman like his uncle: just loves it. In fact," she could hear him chuckle and imagined him stroking his graying moustache in his characteristic manner, "He can bait the hooks faster than either one of us and landed almost every fish he caught. The only thing he's a little squeamish on is eating them. He's used to the squared-off-and-in-a-bun variety."

Essie smiled knowingly. "He sounds just like my grand-sons, Will. We might have been the same way had we grown up with fast food."

"Well, Es, I don't want to keep you on the phone long. One of the docs told me it's your birthday tomorrow, so I called to ask you to lunch. I don't plan on going into the office for the rest of the week, but could come by and pick you up."

Essie wrinkled her nose and suppressed a small sigh. She hated to refuse him again. "I'm so sorry, Will, but the day is already filled. I do appreciate your offer, though." She thought of adding "I'll take a rain check," but didn't. She could hear him let out a slow, resigned breath. She felt guilty about turning him down again, especially since she had no really good reason for doing so. He was a kind, interesting man.

"It is rather last minute," he said, interrupting her thoughts. "Bob raved about that new place downtown and I thought this would be a good time to try it. Maybe another time." She heard the familiar, easy confidence come back into his voice. "We'll get together yet! Have a nice birthday; I'll probably see you Monday at work."

Essie bid Will a good night and hung up the telephone. Her gaze drifted to the picture on the mantle. It was hard to believe Ed had been gone for five years. She had always thought they would spend their "silver years" in some retire-ment center, living out the last of their eighty or ninety years doing volunteer work and witnessing the birth of some of their great-grandchildren. But here she was a widow, almost fifty-five years old to the day, with no thought of retirement in her head or in the near future. And here was another man asking her out, again, for a date. A date! Her granddaughters were dating, for heaven's sake! Her granddaughters! What did one do on a date these days? What would they do? Would conversation come as easily as it did in the office or at lunch with a group of people? No, she decided, she guessed she just wasn't ready to be a "swinging single" or whatever dating people called themselves now. She gave her cat a pat on the head as he returned to the chair and she rose to go to bed.

"No, Franklin, I'm just not ready yet. . . ." She glanced in the mirror with a yawn. What did those granddaughters of hers have in mind this time? A homemade cake? She hoped it wouldn't be another iguana like they bought their mother a few years back. That had been their worst "gift" ever!

After a long, busier-than-usual day at the office, Essie met her daughter and granddaughters at the mall as planned. She had to admit having little appetite after the girls at the office had taken her out for lunch. Janell took a final sip of her coffee as the four of them got up from the table.

"It's time, Mom," Jan said as she gathered up her purse and the bill. Kari and Kristi, her daughters of seventeen and fifteen, each grabbed one of Essie's hands.

"Come on, Gram!" said Kari. "It's time for the best birthday present you ever got! By the way, Gram, you don't have a weak stomach, do you?" Essie stopped short, but the girls just pulled her back into motion.

"What's that supposed to mean?" asked Essie, noting her diminishing excitement about this so-called unique gift.

"I mean," Kari swung her hand buoyantly, "did you ever go to the doctor's office after lunch and have to get a shot?" Essie stopped solidly this time, Kristi giggling at her older sister. Janell almost ran into all three of them as she put away her wallet.

"Are you getting me inoculated to take a trip to Africa or something?"

This time the girls stopped. Essie had to wait for their laughter—she privately labeled it "guffaws"—to end. Janell locked her arm in her mother's, allowing the girls to lead the way.

"That was good, Mom," she laughed. "You have almost as much imagination as the girls."

"THIS IS IT!" Kari announced with her sister smiling triumphantly beside her. Essie looked at the small booth before her; it took a split second for the sign to register: "Piercing Emporium." Each of the girls took one of her hands again, both talking at once in an excited staccato.

"Come on, Gram. No more clip-ons for you!"

"Nope, this is the real thing!"

"You'll look smashing, Gram!"

"Yeah! You'll be begging us to bring you back to get them double-pierced in a month!"

"We've already picked out your starter set—even Dad likes them! And they don't look old-ladyish either!"

"Isn't this great, Gram? You provide the ears, we provide the earrings!"

Essie was incredulous as she looked at her daughter who stood with arms folded. Janell gave her a shrug and a teasing smile. "Told you it was an original idea," she said.

"I don't know about this. . ." Essie hedged.

Jan took her arm again and gently pushed her towards the partial door held open by the salesclerk. "Nonsense. You should have done this years ago. Time to catch up with the present, Granny. You won't regret it."

Kari reached over the counter, holding out a delicate pair of simple gold earrings. To Essie they looked like miniature torture devices for unsuspecting grandmothers. "Aren't these neat, Gram?" asked Kari.

"This is your starter set," Kristi went on to explain. "They'll tell you how to take care of them and everything!" Essie wondered what the "everything" meant, but held her peace. She hardly heard anything the salesclerk said.

"If this hurts," she said menacingly to her granddaughters, "I'll scream and cry and embarrass you all to death." Kristi only giggled.

"It won't hurt, Grandma."

"That's not exactly what you said earlier." Essie braced herself as the stranger marked her earlobes.

"Don't be a chicken, Gram. There's nothing to it," Kari said matter-of-factly. Then, with a coy grin, "Besides, we wouldn't stand by and let our Gram be tortured, would we?"

Essie was about to reply when the clerk said "Here we go!" at the same time Essie heard a crunch or click. Her kinswomen all clapped.

"One down and one to go, Gram!"

"Almost done, Grandma. It wasn't bad, was it?"

Jan just stood beaming, saying nothing. Another click and it was done.

"There you go," said the piercer, handing her a mirror. "Want to take a look?" Essie took the mirror, amazed that there wasn't blood everywhere. She looked up at Jan and the girls.

"Ladies, you were right. They look good. Thank you for such a nice, surprise gift." Kari and Kristi circled Essie like two buzzards as Jan paid the bill.

"Let me see up close, Gram. . .smashing! Just awesome!" gushed Kari.

"Do you really like them, Grandma?" asked Kristi. "Are you glad we got them for you?"

"Yes, I do and am," Essie smiled. "But I'm glad you two will be staying overnight to tell me just what I'm supposed to do again."

"We will, Gram. There's nothing to it."

"Hey, Kari, is that Chad over there?" Kari's eyes followed Kristi's gaze.

"Yes!" She waved back as the group of teenagers saw them and started towards them. Kari turned to her mother. "Can we go talk to Mindy and the rest of the kids for a minute, Mom?" Jan had barely given her answer in the affirmative when the two girls were off to chat with their friends. Jan turned to her mother.

"So much for the excitement over your new look. How about a yogurt cone?"

It was midnight before Essie climbed into bed that night and she was up by seven the next day. She let the girls sleep in, but they were rummaging through the attic by eleven that morning. Every item Essie thought suitable for the garage sale, the girls claimed to be a family treasure or priceless antique. Essie scratched her head after a couple of hours at their project. It didn't look as though she would be getting rid of much with these two misers around! She bundled up one plastic bag of incontestable garbage.

"You girls about had enough? How about a sandwich and I'll take you home?" Both girls nodded their agreement. This attic digging was beginning to get a little boring. As a newly acquired habit, Essie reached up and gave her new earrings a small turn. Kristi, never one to miss anything, grinned at her grandmother.

"Do you still like 'em, Grandma?" she asked as they made their way to the kitchen.

"I sure do, honey. I might go to the store later today and start getting some ideas for some other pairs. You know, I'll also be able to sell all my clips at the garage sale. That should pay for some new pairs."

"Great idea, Gram," Kari agreed as she followed behind her sister. Kari wrinkled her nose as she looked inside the refrigerator. "Hey, Gram, can we stop for burgers instead? I've got some money from baby-sitting the other night."

"I suppose so, Kari. But you girls worked hard this morning, so I'll treat. I'll grab my purse and we can be off."

It was a solid twenty minutes before the three of them left the house; Kari wasn't about to appear in public without a "quick touch-up" as she called it. She curled her hair, put on fresh makeup, and changed clothes. Kristi was not allowed makeup yet, but she too combed her hair for several minutes and changed her clothes. Essie looked down at her favorite gardening jeans. They were passable and so was she.

They finally climbed into the car and soon pulled into Essie's least favorite fast-food spot. A cup of coffee and a small box of cookies made up her lunch. She and Kristi sat down to eat; Kari had run into some friends and sat with them at another table. Essie asked a blessing on the food and looked up to watch her youngest granddaughter dive into her large bag of french fries.

"I'm not always sure it's right to ask a blessing over this food," Essie mumbled as she slowly opened her cookies. Kristi took a big bite of her sandwich and looked across the table at her grandmother.

"Why? It's good!" she managed to say between bites. Essie was just about to venture a reply when she was interrupted.

"Hi, ladies. Got room for one more?"

Essie smiled her surprise and recognition at her accountant friend. She slid over to make room for Will. "We certainly do, Will. Have a seat."

The tall man lowered himself into the booth and removed his sunglasses after setting his tray down. "Have you met my granddaughter Kristi, Will? I think she may have come to the office a few times when you were around. Kris, this is Mr. Davidson," Essie said by way of introduction.

Will nodded and smiled kindly at Kristi. "I may have met you once, Kristi, but I'm not sure. At any rate, it's my pleasure. Are you and your grandmother spending the day together?" he asked.

"No, Mr. Davidson. My sister and I spent the night at Grandma's and we stopped here for lunch on the way home."

"Kristi's sister, Kari, is the blond over there in the blue shirt," Essie indicated with a glance in Kari's direction. "She spotted some friends when we came, although I doubt it was by coincidence they were here, so Kris and I were left on our own. What are you about today?"

Will finished a long drink of pop before answering. "Mike's dad, the dad of your youngest boss, that is, and I went golfing. Great day for golf; can't say my game was so great." Essie gave Kari a stern look from across the room as the talking and laughing from Kari's group got louder. Will's question brought her attention back to themselves.

"How was your birthday, Esther? Did you do anything special?" She raised an eyebrow at Kristi who grinned back at her.

"Kris, Kari, and their mother and I went out for supper last night and then the girls took me to get my gift, which I'm wearing even as we speak."

Will appraised her quickly, but was not struck with anything out of the ordinary. He swallowed the last of his hastily eaten sandwich and looked from Essie to Kristi and back again.

"Well, you've got me. New shirt? New hairstyle?" Kristi answered before Essie opened her mouth.

"We got her pierced earrings, Mr. Davidson. Show him, Grandma." Essie turned her head to face Will, who smiled his approval. "Don't you think they look neat, Mr. David-son?" asked Kristi.

"They sure do look neat, Kristi," his blue eyes twinkled as he regarded Essie with a teasing grin. Essie felt a little self-conscious all of a sudden and could feel the color rising to her cheeks. "Very flattering, Mrs. Gregory. Was it painful?" he asked.

"Not really, but I'm afraid we made quite a scene at the mall. It was certainly a birthday surprise."

"Grandma, can I get a shake?" Kristi asked, sliding out of her seat. Essie gave Kristi some money and watched as her granddaughter greeted two girls who came in as she was ordering her milk shake.

"Was this something your granddaughters thought of?" Will asked, placing an elbow on the table and smoothing a corner of his moustache.

Essie finished her coffee and shook her head. "All by themselves! The two of them always come up with the unex-pected. All four of my grandkids are special, Will. I wouldn't mind four or fourteen more!" Will looked wistful for a moment before answering.

"I can understand that even though I don't have any kids or grandkids. I like to spend time with my nephews and nieces. I admit to sometimes wishing I had grand-children." He seemed pensive and Essie ventured a question that she had wondered about since knowing Will, but had never asked.

"Why is it you never got married, Will? There are very few bachelors from our generation, you know." He nodded his agreement and cradled his chin on his hand.

"That's for sure. I've always been the odd man out, but it never bothered me much for the most part. I don't know, Esther. The proverbial right girl just never came along, I guess." He looked at her intently and then straightened up with a quick stretch, bringing his right hand down gently to rest on hers.

"So, what do you say, my friend from the office? How about breaking down and going to the symphony with me tonight? I've got great tickets and this is the last performance before the summer."

Essie was a little taken back by the quick change in the conversation. She was very conscious of his hand on hers, but saw nothing in his eyes that she had not seen before. . . unless it was a tenderness that she had never taken the time to notice before today. Will had always struck her as self-assured, in control, and confident without being overbearing or arrogant. She had always thought of him as more of a public relations man than a bookworm poring over columns of numbers. Perhaps she was really seeing him here in a fast-food restaurant—of all places!—for the first time.

"Well. . ." She hesitated and out of her new habit found her free hand touching her earlobe and tiny earring again. She scolded herself silently. *What am I thinking anyway? Why not go out on a date with a man I have known and admired since our first meeting?* She gave him a big smile of resolve.

"I'd love to, Will. Just tell me the time."

He couldn't repress a sudden chuckle. "Esther Gregory,

I never thought I'd hear an acceptance from you! In case I never get the chance again, we're going to do it up right: dinner at six, the symphony at eight, and dessert to follow. Sound good? If all goes well, maybe a quick nine holes of golf tomorrow. What do you say?"

Essie laughed quietly and pursed her lips. "You're on, Mr. Davidson. I'll be ready by 5:30." Will got up from the table just as the two girls returned.

"Ready to go, Grandma?" asked Kristi, offering a sip of her shake to her sister. Kari looked at Will with a vague sense of recognition.

"Kari, this is Mr. Davidson. He works at the building where I work."

"I think Gram did introduce us before, Mr. Davidson. Hi."

"Hi, Kari. I think we've met before, too." Will opened the door as they all walked outside. Essie followed her granddaughters to the car and waved good-bye to Will.

"Thank you, Will. I'll see you later this afternoon," she called.

Will put on his sunglasses and walked briskly to his car, smiling back at Essie. "Five-thirty sharp, I'll be there, Esther. Have a vase ready for some flowers, too."

Essie got into the car after the girls. She couldn't help smiling to herself as she started the engine. She glanced quickly at herself in the rearview mirror and pushed back a stray curl. Maybe this date business wouldn't be as awful as she had feared.

"You going to see Mr. Davidson later, Gram?" asked

Kari, checking her hair in a mirror retrieved from her purse.

"Yes, honey. We're going to dinner and then the symphony." Neither of her granddaughters appeared to think the announcement anything out of the ordinary. Kari dropped her mirror back into her purse and Kristi blew a bubble with her gum.

"Neat, Gram," Kari said, snapping her seat belt into place.

"Yeah," rejoined Kristi, looking out the side window. "He seems like a kinda neat guy. I don't know about that symphony part, though."

"You would probably like it if you ever went, Kris. Maybe I'll take you in a few years." Essie glanced knowingly at her granddaughter and gave her new earrings a twist. She let out a quiet, confident sigh. She would enjoy this date tonight, even if it was a date. Will was, after all, a "kinda neat guy."

CHAPTER 7

A Time to Begin

Will Davidson changed his tie for the third time. He grinned at his reflection in the mirror. You'd think this was the first date of his life. Here he was sixty years old and feeling like he was sixteen. *Yep, this tie will do it,* he thought. He gave one more touch to his graying mustache and patted down a stubborn silver hair over his right ear. Tonight was his first date with Esther. His first real date with Esther—no group get-together or collection of a dozen or so matched and mismatched people. Just him and her. How long had he been trying to get a date with this woman? One year? Two? He grabbed the box of flowers on the table and headed out the door to his car.

During his drive to Esther's house Will recalled his life as a bachelor. He had come close to getting married once, but that had been years ago. He glanced in the rearview mirror and once again smoothed down the corner of his mustache. How long had Esther been a widow? Probably about four years, he guessed. He didn't remember when he had made his decision: for this woman he would leave bachelorhood behind and do so gladly. He had thought about it, prayed about it, and probably dreamed about it too. Now was the time for action. He had asked her out numerous times, but had never pushed. He was confident about someday sharing his life with her. He didn't want to force his way into a more intimate place in her life prematurely. So, he had settled for group lunches and informal chats at the office. He had kept asking her out every so often. She had always said "no." Her refusals were always kind, sometimes even hesitant, but refusals nonetheless. Until today. He smiled as he turned into her driveway.

"You won't get away, Miss Esther," he said aloud. "Your days are numbered and you'll be changing your name before those beautiful green eyes of yours see what's coming."

"Come in, Will." Esther's smile was warm as she greeted the tall man before her.

"These are for you, Miss Esther, just as promised," Will said as he held the box of flowers out to her. He didn't miss the slight blush on her cheeks or the sparkle in her incredibly green eyes.

"They're lovely, Will. Thank you. How did you know I like yellow roses the best?" He followed her into the kitchen as she stood on tiptoe to get a vase down from the cupboard.

"Just a guess," he answered, easily reaching the vase for her. She thanked him again and went to the counter to arrange the roses in the vase. "Your house is nice, Esther. Is a lot of work for you?"

"Sometimes. But a neighbor boy takes care of the lawn for me in the warm months and shovels the drive and sidewalks in the winter. I've thought about a condo or an apartment, but moving sounds like too much work. You have a condo, don't you?" The two of them returned to the living room, Esther still arranging the roses to her satisfaction.

"Yes," Will answered. "I haven't owned a house for a long time." He helped her put on her light coat and noticed she smelled fresh and not like perfume. He liked that. How many women had he dated whose cologne gave him a pounding headache? Too many, he concluded. She turned to face him, murmuring another "thank you" for the fragrant roses.

"You look beautiful, Esther," he said. "Ready to go?" She picked up her purse and was about to reply when the telephone rang. She gave him a rueful smile.

"Thought I was. Give me a minute." She picked up the receiver and motioned for Will to have a seat.

"Hello, dear," she answered into the telephone. "It's my son," she mouthed silently to Will. "I was just on my way out the door," she continued into the receiver. "No," she replied in answer to a question. She turned her head to face Will again and gave him an apologetic smile.

"Do you remember the accountant from the firm down the hall where I work? He does our books every year?" She paused briefly. "Yes, Will Davidson. We were just on our way out the door for dinner and the symphony."

Will picked up a magazine and started to whistle a tune. He gave Esther a self-assured smile and a wink. The whole family might as well know his interest in their mother from the beginning. He didn't think Esther dated much, if ever, so this might be a real surprise for her son. Esther turned from

Will again and laughed at some remark her son made.

"Am I expected to call and report in tomorrow?" Will heard her ask. There was a brief pause and Esther turned to roll her eyes at Will. "Very funny," she said to her son. "I'll call you tomorrow. G'night, dear." She hung up the telephone and went to the door. "Let's hurry before it rings again," she said to Will. "It seems we're the talk of the family tonight."

"Is that so?" He helped her into the car.

"Yes. It seems my daughter learned of our date from my granddaughters. She in turn called one of her sisters, who called my son, and on it goes."

"We'll just have to be sure to give them something worth talking about," Will said. "Now, let's get something to eat."

Their dinner was a quiet, enjoyable affair. Conversation came easily and Will was pleased that Esther talked to him so freely. She seemed a little self-conscious and shy at first, but soon they were talking as naturally as they did at work. They learned more about each other in the course of an hour over their meal than they had in the few years they had known each other. They shared laughs about mutual acquaintances at work, their golf games, and their families. In their serious moments they spoke of their faith in Jesus Christ and how they each became Christians. They ended up leaving the restaurant in a hurry to be on time for the concert.

As the evening wore on Will found himself growing more pensive and less talkative, even during the intermission. He watched Esther unobtrusively throughout the orchestra's performance. As he followed Esther's emotions by watching her face, he thought that this was a good place to fall in love. How could he help it? The music was beautiful, Esther was beautiful, and the evening was turning out even better than he had imagined.

Esther turned to him suddenly. She didn't seem to notice he had been watching her for the previous several minutes. She touched his arm lightly and brought her head close to his to be heard.

"Isn't it lovely, Will?" she asked. "The beauty of the music is absolutely wonderful." She closed her eyes contentedly with a sigh and turned her attention back to the performance. Will took her hand in his and raised it to his lips for a gentle kiss. He wasn't sure she even noticed. When he brought her hand down in his to rest on his knee, she did not pull away and even entwined her fingers with his. He turned his own attention back to the music with an almost imperceptible shake of his head. He had better pay some attention; the tickets had cost him plenty!

Esther declined dessert after the concert, but invited Will in for some coffee. She was so quiet during their ride home he began to wonder if his small caress had been perceived as presumptuous. He hoped not. He had found not touching her difficult. He had enjoyed being with Esther and told her so. He liked her genuine smiles that were just for him. He liked being two together instead of one alone. And he liked it a lot.

"How about some decaf, Will?" she asked as they entered her house once again. Will smoothed his hair back and suppressed an unbidden yawn that suddenly came upon him.

"I'd like to say 'yes,' Esther, but I'll have to take a rain check." The feelings he was experiencing were beginning to irritate him. The truth was, he didn't trust himself to stay until he had a better handle on his emotions. He was afraid he would say or do something stupid. He found himself looking at her and thinking about her in ways that told him his hormones were getting ahead of his good sense. Plus he was tired and "tired" made him feel vulnerable. He didn't like feeling vulnerable.

"Are you sure?" she asked brightly. "It's still early. . . ."

Will walked to the door and exhaled slowly before answering. *Actually,* he thought, *it's kind of humorous.* Esther probably had no idea what was going through his mind. How could she? He was the one having all these wild thoughts and could hardly believe it himself! He answered her in his usual quiet, controlled way.

"No, thanks, Es. Are we still on for golf tomorrow?"

"Sure. Why don't you come early? I make a mean omelet and we can walk off the calories during our round of golf."

"Sounds good," he replied. "I'll be here about nine." He thought better of kissing her good night and simply laid his hand against the softness of her cheek. "Good night. I'll see you in the morning." He was surprised when she touched her hand to his and turned her head to touch her lips to the palm of his hand. He could feel his pulse quicken and at the same time told himself that he was acting like a fool. "There's no fool like a old fool" immediately popped into his head and he couldn't agree more.

The next morning Will spent the same as he had done every morning for more years than he cared to count. He was up before six, fixed himself a strong cup of coffee, worked on whatever part of the Bible he was currently studying, and then prayed. His praying this morning was different than other mornings, however. For so many months he had had this quiet confidence about winning Esther's heart in a matter of days. Now he realized his heart was the one that had been won and he hadn't even seen it coming. He prayed for wisdom, for sensitivity, for. . .her to be his. Afterwards he scratched his early morning's growth of beard and sauntered to the shower, still pensive.

He thought again of a portion of scripture he had read a few weeks back and retraced his steps to the den to look at it once more. He found it in the Book of Proverbs:

> *There are three things that are too amazing for me,*
> *four that I do not understand: the way of an eagle in*
> *the sky, the way of a snake on a rock, the way of a ship*
> *on the high seas, and the way of a man with a maiden.*

He closed his Bible with a rueful smile. He himself had never had a wife, let alone a few hundred of them. Yet Solomon, the husband of hundreds, apparently had not understood this courtship stuff any better than he did!

"Right on time!" Esther said as she opened the door for Will a few hours later. He surprised himself—and probably her as well—by kissing her lightly.

If Esther was taken aback by his sudden demonstration of affection, she didn't show it, except for a sudden flush in her cheeks which Will found pleasing. He knew this day was going to be great—no matter how he golfed!

As it turned out, he was right. Their breakfast was another quietly pleasant time of small talk and getting to know more about one another. At the golf course they were paired with another couple. During the course of the game they learned that the other man was related to Esther's employer. They were fairly well-matched in their golfing skill and had such a good time together that they exchanged telephone numbers at the end of their round and talked of golfing together on purpose another time.

Back at Will's condo, Esther and Will relaxed on his patio with some iced tea. The distant whine of a lawnmower reminded Will that spring was rapidly revitalizing his own lawn. Esther looked around the small backyards, somewhat privatized by split rail fencing and forsythia bushes, the latter already becoming a brilliant yellow.

"This is nice, Will. How long have you lived here?" she asked.

"I bought this condo about six years ago. I can walk to church or the library from here and take the bus to work if I don't feel like driving. I've got great neighbors, too. Hey. . ." he pushed his sunglasses up on top of his head. "How about coming to church with me tomorrow?"

Esther pulled off one of her shoes and began rubbing her foot. "I'd like to, but I have some commitments at my own church. Want to come to Grace with me?" she asked.

"Only if you join me for lunch afterwards. What do you say?"

"That sounds nice." Esther reached down and pulled her shoe back on.

"Is that a 'yes'?" he asked, taking another sip of his iced tea.

"That's a 'yes'," she smiled in return.

They sat on the patio for several seconds in silence. Will regarded Esther quietly, wondering what she was thinking. She rose and reached for his empty glass. He opened the door for her and followed her into the kitchen. Esther set the glasses on the counter and turned to find herself facing Will. He took both her hands in his.

"You know, Esther, you may have sealed your fate when you finally consented to go out with me last night."

"How so?" she asked.

"You may be stuck with me for a long time," he said. He gently pulled her into his embrace. This time Will did not give Esther a quick kiss. He warmed to her return kiss and the feel of her arms wrapping around him. He held her closely after kissing her, relishing the fragrance of her hair and her head against his shoulder. It felt good to be kissing Esther. Finally. *And better yet to be kissed back!* he thought with a grin.

"What are you thinking just now?" she asked.

He chuckled and touched a kiss to her forehead. "I was thinking I might need to get a prescription from your boss the doctor to return my suddenly elevated blood pressure back down to normal. I've waited a long time for this, Esther," he said truthfully. "I can't believe I'm finally here alone with you! That I have you all to myself!"

"And I never thought I'd find myself in the arms of a man again," she replied, smoothing the collar of his shirt. "And enjoying it so much," she finished with a shy smile.

They walked to the living room, Will with his arm draped gently across Esther's shoulders. They sat on the sofa together and Will kept her close beside him in the circle of his arm.

"I can't tell you how much I've enjoyed these last twenty-four hours, Esther."

"Me too," she said simply. "But. . ."

Will felt a sense of discomfort at that one word. "But. . . what?" he asked, somewhat hesitantly.

Esther fingered a curl near her cheek. "Do you think. . . uh. . .do you think. . ." she repeated, "things may be moving a little too fast here?" She didn't give him a chance to answer. "I mean, I haven't dated in a long time, Will. Although we've known each other for a long time, this has been uncomfortable for me—even now." She looked at him with a strained smile. "Am I making any sense?" She stood up and went back into the kitchen. "This is ridiculous," she said more to herself than to him. "Want some more iced tea?"

Will leaned back against the sofa and absently stroked his mustache. *So now what, Casanova?* he asked himself. What had changed the sweet moment of intimacy they had just shared? *Should I answer her question? Give her a week to think about us?* What was there to think about? They had shared all of one kiss, one date, and one round of golf together!

Esther returned, handing him another glass of iced tea. Her look said: your turn. Will took the beverage he hadn't asked for and thought for a few more seconds. He was going to be frank with Esther. It had been his way in life and in business. It was him and he wasn't going to change now.

"Esther, I've been asking you out for a long time. I'm sixty years old and I'm not getting younger. I've invested a lot of thought and prayer into a relationship with you. So, for me anyway, no. I don't think things are moving too fast. But I won't push you. If my sixty years have taught me anything, it's patience. I want you to know, however," he held her eyes with his, "that I'm in this for the long haul—unless you put a stop to it."

Esther smiled at him and surprised him by touching her fingers to his temple, smoothing back the hair above his right ear. "You're as forthright as ever, Will. One of the things I've always admired about you." She held his gaze evenly with her own and brought her lips to his cheek. "I need to get home," she said. "The laundry is not going to do itself. . . ."

Will felt as though the conversation had ended in the middle, with him not knowing where he stood in Esther's estimation—or where they stood in Esther's estimation. He decided she needed some time to think. She rose and he stood as well.

"Leave the glasses. I'll take care of them later," he said.

During the drive back to Esther's, they talked about their golf game and the previous night's concert, but nothing about them. Will let it go. Obviously Esther didn't want to discuss it further for now. Once they got to Esther's and Will had put away her golf clubs, they stood in the garage for a few more minutes to talk.

"Should I just meet you at your church in the morning?" he asked.

"I've been thinking about what you said back at your condo," Esther replied, not answering his question. "Would you like to come back tonight? Watch a video? Have some popcorn? Talk about tomorrow? Talk about. . .us?" She looked up at him almost coyly.

Will's mind was as puzzled as he was sure his face must be. Was this the same woman who thought things were moving too quickly minutes ago?

"Well, sure!" he said. "Unless you want to go to a movie. . ."

"No, I think not. I'd rather it just be the two of us: no waitresses, no audience and orchestra, no other golfers. We can talk as much—or as little—as we want. In fact," she said, leading the way back to his car, "why don't you just get a video, change clothes if you want, and come back for supper?"

"Are you sure? Don't do this for me, Esther, unless it's what you want to do. I have the tenacity of a bulldog when I set my sights on something. In this case," he hesitated only briefly, "that 'something' is you."

"I've had such a marvelous time with you that I'm not ready for it to end," she said quietly. "And suddenly, tomorrow sounds a long time away."

"How 'bout if I get us some Chinese food?" he asked. "I could be back by seven or so."

"Can you make it six?" she asked, walking with him back to his car.

"Won't change your mind? I'll bring flowers again," he said with a teasing smile.

"I won't change my mind. And you don't need to bring flowers. Just bring yourself." She lifted her face for a kiss. Will obliged her with just that before getting into his car.

"I might be early," he said with a glance at his watch.

"I'll be ready," she grinned. "After all, like you said, we're not getting any younger."

They both heard her telephone ringing and Will started his car.

"Later," he said, smoothing down a corner of his mustache.

As he pulled out of the driveway he saw Esther wave at him from inside the screen door, holding her portable telephone to her ear. He waved back with a confident smile and a prayer of thanks in his heart. He would bet that was his future stepson on the telephone!

CHAPTER 8

The Longest Wait

I'm sitting here on the edge of the bed, keeping my eyes closed against the bright sunlight streaming in through the window. My mother's frequent admonitions to me when I was young keep coming to mind: Remember your place. Don't be too quick to get angry. Don't fall too hard when you fall in love. "In short," she would conclude with a sniff and a lift of her head, "keep your head above water."

Like my siblings, I trusted my mother's sage advice. We all knew she spoke from a true, loving heart. As a mother of somewhat advanced years when she reared us, we knew she spoke with wisdom that came from long experience. I know it was a wisdom not many younger mothers often have. Yet, did she really make it clear to me how very powerful love could be? How compelling and engulfing love could be when there was a bright, attentive, and loving Joey in my world?

Joey. Just his name makes my heart beat faster. I can't just sit or lie down when I think of him. I want to run, to jump, to let anyone know who will listen that I love this boy of mine! Who would have thought a few short years ago that our somewhat tenuous beginning would blossom into this all-consuming passion?

And passion it is. Except for the Glorious One who made me, I value Joey above everyone and everything else. I live for him. I would die for him. I think he would do the same for me. Our love is very strong; it is very powerful! But it is sweet too. . .and it is so very real.

We were both very young when we met. For whatever reasons, I suppose we were even afraid of each other. I was in a new city, far from all that was familiar to me. I was timid, probably shaken, and hesitant to make the acquaintance of this young man with the stick-straight blond hair. His hair was so unlike mine, which is forever curly, tangled, in my eyes. . .but Joey's eyes! I had never seen such huge orbs! Big, bright, twinkling, and bluer than the sky on a clear summer day! I have often since wondered if big eyes are in proportion to the bigness of one's heart, for Joey has a big heart full of love for me. It wasn't very long before this boy with the huge, eager eyes and I were on a first-name basis and playmates from sunrise to sunset.

When did I realize we were more than playmates? When is the sunset most beautiful? When is the autumn its most aromatic? I can no more answer these last two questions than the first. I do recall, however, a day both of us were lying in the grass. It was a cool day, not quite spring. The sun was delightfully warm on our faces in spite of the low temperature. The penetrating warmth soaked through our winter coats. I gently touched the tip of my nose to Joey's cheek and he draped his arm around me, drawing me even closer. I remember thinking at that moment: how long have I loved this wonderful man-child with the laughing eyes? I didn't know then, and I don't know now. I can't remember when we didn't love one another—except, perhaps, that first day.

But now he's gone. He's been gone for many sunrises and sunsets. I'm trying hard not to "mope" as my mother would have called it, but my life is all wrapped up in Joey's and Joey isn't here. No matter how tiring a day he has, he always brightens to see me. He makes time for me. He teases me about my curls, but he always cushions his teasing with some surprise treat or a simple: "You're the best, Frances." It isn't much, but he means it and I know it. He didn't tell me he was leaving, however. He didn't say where he was going, or even that he was going at all. I keep watching out this window for some sign of him, but it's been many days and he has not been here. I've lost my appetite. I haven't been doing my regular daily running. I've been doing nothing at all. So, I guess I am "moping" and moping with a big "M." Nothing is in balance and everything is out of place.

I've tried to amuse myself with other people, or get into some mischief by myself. But like I said, nothing is quite right and I simply don't have any motivation to do much more than stare out the window, waiting and watching for Joey. When Joey is here, he always has good ideas. His ideas are creative, ingenious, and a lot more fun than those of most boys! Sometimes his ideas have gotten us into trouble, but not everyone sees things the way Joey and I do. (They don't have as much fun as we do either.) But without Joey there is no fun.

How deserted the street looks outside. From up here I can see most of the street in both directions, but I don't see the one I want to see. The sun must be warm because I've seen one or two kids riding by on their bicycles. Others are whizzing down the street on in-line skates. I've got to snap out of these doldrums—try to eat a good breakfast tomorrow and take a long run in the late morning. Yes, that's what I'll do. Eat well. Run long. With or without Joey, I'll do it. But I'll do it. . .tomorrow. . . .

What's that?

Is that the car he gets around in sometimes? Very unladylike, I crane my neck to get a better look out the window. It is him! He's here!

I run down the stairs two at a time, but Joey beats me to the door as he always does, bursting into the room with energy and exuberance.

"Frannie! I'm home!" He kneels down to scoop me up and I fly into his arms, knocking him over and licking his face until I think my tongue will fall off. His laughter fills the once-empty house and my whole being.

"Frances," he laughs, his eyelashes closed against my kisses. "You're the best! The best dog a boy ever had!"

And everything is right again.

CHAPTER 9

The Loss

I've got a full day at the office, honey, but Ken is on call this week, so we should be able to quietly discuss your first day back at work when I get home tonight. Are you ready for it?" Luke asked, placing his coffee cup in the sink. Julie absently pushed the last of her grapefruit around the bowl. She smiled at him with a shrug of her shoulders.

"I'd better be. I'm expected come nine o'clock. Besides, we can't afford for me to be off any longer." She looked around at the small kitchen of their small apartment. How could so little living area cost so much? "Come here a second; you've got a piece of lint or something on the back of your pant leg."

"Sure. . .any excuse to get fresh," he teased.

"Don't flatter yourself," she replied, pulling off a small piece of lint and following it with a love pat. She stood to put the rest of her uneaten grapefruit in the refrigerator. Luke pushed her back down onto her chair.

"No, you don't. You finish your breakfast—all of it," he ordered. "I'm back to my normal weight—you need to get back to yours. You're as skinny as Mrs. Day. If either of you get any skinnier I won't be able to find you." Luke gave Julie a coffee-scented kiss and kept her face lifted towards his. "Sure you're ready?" he repeated, his loving concern forcing Julie to hold back tears. She nodded and wrapped her arms around his shoulders to avoid his penetrating look. He pulled her to her feet with a return embrace.

"You don't have to go in if you need more time, Jules," he whispered against her hair. "I'll call John and tell him—"

"No, I'll be fine. Come on, you'll be late for work." She patted his back and released him. He picked up his keys from the counter and walked to the door. He turned back going out and pointed his finger.

"The rest of the grapefruit, Mrs. Vincent," he said and was gone. Julie obediently picked up her bowl and walked to the living room window, eating the few grapefruit sections that remained. She waved at Luke as he got into the car and then drove towards the street. She walked back to the kitchen and finished rinsing the remaining dishes. She could hear the sounds of their neighbors above, below, and beside them through the paper-thin walls. She never heard the only neighbor she knew well on the one side of them: Mrs. Day. Neither she nor Luke could ever call her Leona; it didn't fit her twinkling eyes. She was a fragile, petite woman, just as Luke had said, but her sharp wit and no-nonsense demeanor left no room for anyone to notice her size. Julie smiled to herself and walked towards the bathroom. But her eyes went to the door at the end of the short, narrow hall and, as she had done almost every morning for the last eight months, she continued on to the bedroom at the end of the hall.

She opened the door and stood, taking it all in again. She let her hand glide over the rough edge of the used crib before she sat in the rocker. She smiled to herself. Her rambunctious niece, long past the age of diapers and cribs, had doubtless chewed those little dents in the crib railing with her own teeth. Julie and Luke would have liked to have purchased a new crib, but it simply wasn't in the budget.

"This would have been your room, little Luke," she said aloud and began rocking, rocking, her eyes closed and the familiar ache returning to her heart and stomach. She hadn't had any of those horrible flashbacks lately to the day she lost her baby, but today she was remembering everything as if she were a detached observer—watching the events, but not feeling the torrent of emotions through which she and Luke had passed that February day and the horrible days that followed.

She had just finished her day of teaching and was getting ready to go home. She had patted her rounding belly, glad for the presence of this child for whom they had prayed and waited. She wanted nothing more than to get home and get her feet up. Even though she was only six months along, she was already having problems with her feet swelling after standing before her class all day. She felt a little crampy, but assumed it was more "practice labor," as her obstetrician called it. Getting her ready for the real thing when it came along.

By the time she had driven home, she was getting scared. It didn't seem right; the cramps were more regular and harder than she'd ever had before. Fortunately, Luke was home early that day. He had been so calm. He had grabbed her books and purse, thrown them on the chair, and helped her to the sofa.

"I'm so scared, Luke," she had said, her lips trembling and her eyes watering. "It's so early. . . !"

He had shushed her with the touch of his hand while he dialed her doctor's office with the other. All she remembered about the short trip to the hospital was Luke's quiet talking. She clutched his hand tightly, trying to pray, trying to focus, trying to remember what chances a baby had of surviving if she delivered more than three months early. She wanted to think, but she was so terrified that all she could do was count, breathe, and nod at Luke, trying to reassure him that she was doing okay, but all the time feeling she wasn't.

She was relieved to find her obstetrician waiting for them in the emergency room. Julie had liked Sharon Burke the first time she had met her. She had never been to a woman doctor before, but was at ease with Dr. Burke from her first office visit onward. After Dr. Burke's standard "How are you doing, Julie?" Julie noticed that for the first time her physician didn't wait for an answer. She was putting on gloves and giving orders to the nurse nearby. The nurse had helped Julie undress from the waist down and get up on the examining table.

"I'm going to check you quickly, Julie, to see if you're dilating. Has your water broken yet?"

"No. . .is the baby going to be okay? Where is Luke?"

Julie was trembling and more frightened than she had ever been in her life.

"He's at the desk. He'll be here shortly," Dr. Burke rose from the stool and peeled off her examining gloves. "Get an IV started and get her upstairs ASAP," she said to the nurse before facing Julie. She gave Julie a small smile and patted her hand. "Sorry, we needed to take care of business first. We'll get Luke and I'll tell you what's going on and what we're going to do."

Julie's response was cut short by another sharp contraction. After the pain had passed, Luke was shown into the room while the nurse was starting Julie's IV.

"Come in, Luke. Come here by Julie so I can tell you what we're going to do." Dr. Burke let Luke stand in her place and she went to the other side of the bed to face them both. "Julie is in labor, as you both have figured out, I'm sure. She's dilated five centimeters, which isn't too bad. She's still intact—that is, her bag of waters hasn't broken, which is good. We're going to start a medication to stop the labor, if we can. We'll move you up to OB and do an ultrasound to see just what junior is doing in there. I'll have one of the neonatologists come and talk to you about the little guy inside, but first we need to do all our business stuff, okay? We're going to be long on doing and short on talking until we get the magnesium sulfate going and slow things down. But we'll get you upstairs first and answer the questions as we go." She turned to the nurse. "IV in?" The nurse nodded in the affirmative. "Good. Let's get upstairs so we can get the mag going. I'll see you two in a few minutes," said the doctor and she was out the door.

The next hour was a blur for Julie. She was trying to assimilate all the information being doled out by more people than she could count coming into her room, but she simply couldn't. She would just nod her head as if she understood everything and hold all the tighter to Luke's hand. She was hoping he was getting everything and could sort it all out for her later. The medication didn't seem to be working, and she was having a hard time trying to keep panic from overwhelming her. But she held onto one thing she could assimilate: the newborn specialist said that babies at their baby's gestation had better than an 80 percent chance of survival. She hung onto that, trying to pray, hoping that the few people Luke had been able to call were praying for her. For them. For their baby.

Julie had lost track of time by the time Dr. Burke had come back in after her ultrasound. She noticed that the doctor had changed her clothes and was in hospital garb. Sharon Burke lay her hand on Julie's abdomen and brushed a wet curl off Julie's forehead.

"Well, you two, this is what's what," she began. "The medication isn't working and your labor is still progressing, Julie. So, since it looks as though your son- or daughter-to-be has the strongest will here, we're going to stop the mag and let little Luke or Lucinda make his or her entrance. The neonatologist and the rest of the nursery team will be on hand for the delivery and we'll get this little one off to the best start we can. I don't think you'll be in labor much longer, Julie. Once the mag is off, you'll probably progress rapidly, so

I won't be far away. You can still come into the delivery room, Luke, even though I know you haven't had any classes to speak of yet. Is that what you want to do?"

"Yeah, doc. I'm not squeamish," he said, trying to smile.

"Okay," she said and turned to go. "The IV will stay in, Julie, until after you deliver. You still don't want an epidural?"

"No. . .unless it puts the baby at risk not to have it," she answered.

"No, it doesn't. This guy isn't too big; I think you'll be able to push him out easily and quickly. I'll see you soon, unless you've got any other questions. . ." She hesitated at the door.

"No, thanks, Dr. Burke," Luke answered for the both of them. For the next hour Julie's obstetrical nurse stayed with them, helping Julie breathe and helping Luke help Julie. Julie felt the labor's intensity much more acutely now that the medication had been stopped, but Luke's presence and the quiet, constant encouragement and assurances from her nurse helped her maintain control and follow instructions. She was in the midst of another contraction when it happened.

Pain! Incredible pain shot through her, unlike any of the labor she'd had so far. She couldn't scream, it robbed her of breath. It must have shown on her face because Luke lost his controlled, quiet look. Julie clutched her abdomen, oblivious to her IV or anything else. The pain wouldn't loosen its grip on her. She could see faces around and above her, but the knife within her robbed her of any other sense or feeling. She didn't know if she were dizzy or moving or both—or neither.

She thought she might be screaming now, but she didn't know. Couldn't they stop this pain? What was wrong? Was she dying? Everything was getting black, but the pain was white-hot. People were talking loudly around her; Dr. Burke was talking into her face, but she couldn't hear her. She saw her mouth moving. She must be talking! But what was she saying? Where was Luke? *Dear Jesus, where is Luke? Where are You?*

Her questions stopped. Everything stopped.

Julie woke up. It was quiet. Her throat hurt; it was hard to swallow. The exquisite pain was gone. Now it was dull, almost not there. A face appeared above hers.

"Julie? Wake up, Julie," the face said. The face turned from her and spoke to someone else. "She's waking up, Luke," it said. Luke's face appeared above Julie's. He laid his rough cheek against hers and Julie felt a tear drop onto her face.

"Jules, sweetheart. I love you," he whispered, stroking her hair back from her forehead.

"What happened? Where. . . ?" Julie felt disoriented. The face which had first appeared to her smiled.

"I'm your nurse, Carol. How are you feeling?" Carol asked, and Julie felt the blood pressure cuff tightening on her arm.

"Fair. My. . .our baby. . ." She turned frightened eyes towards Luke. Her new fear raised her level of consciousness. Luke had been crying; she had never seen him cry and it made her cry. "Is he. . .is he. . . ?" She couldn't ask the question she wanted to ask. She saw Luke look at the nurse, Carol, who shook her head affirmatively. Luke wiped the back of his hand across his nose and wound the fingers of his free hand in Julie's hair.

"He's in the newborn intensive care unit, Jules. He's. . . uh. . .he's holding his own," he managed to say, swallowing hard. His eyes filled with tears. "He's beautiful, honey," he said brokenly, sniffing and wiping his eyes and nose with a tissue. "He's got your brown hair. . ." He stopped to get control and was glad the nurse slipped out the door.

"He's alive? He's a him? He's okay?" Now Julie couldn't get all the questions out fast enough. "Can I see him?"

Luke began brushing at Julie's tears with a trembling hand. He swallowed slowly. His eyes were bloodshot. She noticed his neck was red and the veins stood out. He was still struggling for control; she felt suddenly calm. But it was a detached calm, like everything was happening to someone else.

"Well, I. . .he's on a ventilator and stuff and the doctor says. . ."

A sob broke from Luke and he was trembling so that Julie was afraid for him now. "My God," he rolled his reddened eyes up. "Dear God," he repeated between ragged breaths, "I thought I'd lost you, Jules." He laid his head on her breast and wept. His great, convulsing sobs scared her, but she had to know about the baby. She didn't know how she did it, but she kept silent and just held Luke against her until he quieted. After a few minutes he sat up and blew his nose again.

"Please, Luke, tell me about the baby. Is he okay?" she pleaded.

"I've been so worried about you that I only remember

bits and pieces about the baby. Want to go see him? They said once you were awake we could wheel you down there. . . ."

"Yes, please. Call the nurse. I want to see him."

Dr. Burke came into the room just as Luke went towards the door. The young physician was back in her street clothes and had her purse slung over her shoulder. She gave Julie a small, concerned smile.

"How are you doing, Julie?" she asked for the second time that long day. Julie looked at the bag of IV solution hanging above her and for the first time noticed a unit of blood hanging adjacent to it, the tubing dark with the color where it flowed into another taped vein in her other arm.

"Maybe you had better tell me," she answered, still not feeling herself, or strong enough to do anything other than talk.

"You had what we call a placental abruption. The placenta began to tear away from your uterus. Fortunately, you were here and not home, so we were able to get you to surgery quickly. You lost a fair amount of blood in a short time, but this one unit should get you over the hump. We had to do an emergency cesarean section, of course, for your sake and the baby's, so you're going to be sore for a while. You gave us a run for our money, Mrs. Vincent—and about put your poor husband over the brink." She lifted her face to Luke, who was in control of his emotions again, but whose face still showed the signs of his recent tearful outburst. "How are you, Luke? Okay?" He nodded his head, but didn't answer and just placed his hand on Julie's again.

"Is the baby going to be okay? Can I go see him?" Julie's

earlier fear for herself was gone. She wanted to see their son.

"Well, he's had a rough start, but he couldn't get better care anywhere else right now. One of the neonatologists will answer your questions better than I can at this point, Julie. I'll be in to check on you tomorrow. Luke, you take good care of your wife here." She exited with a few more words of instruction and was gone. Carol came back in and began unplugging cords.

"Give me a hand, Luke?" she asked. "Let's go see this little guy."

Julie was wheeled to the newborn intensive care area where an older woman with short, graying hair met them. She introduced herself as their baby's nurse and helped Carol position Julie's bed so that she could peer into the incubator.

"Have you got a name picked out for this little guy yet?" she asked, lifting a quilted cover off the front of the clear plastic rectangle that housed their precious child.

"Lucas. . .Luke Junior," Julie mumbled, looking at her son for the first time. He was so small. . .so skinny. . .so. . . attached to so many things.

Tears came to Julie's eyes again. "Is. . .is he in pain?" she asked.

"No," the nurse reassured her. "He's been quiet and just resting for the last half hour or so. Let me tell you about some of all these gadgets, so they don't frighten you unnecessarily." The nurse continued to talk, but Julie hardly heard her or was conscious of anything or anyone else.

Here he was. Little Luke. He was so tiny. He did have dark brown hair; his fingers and toes were long like Luke's.

He was so perfect—a perfect, miniature little man. In fact, he looked more like a miniature old man than a miniature baby. He wasn't moving; his chest would go up and down with the respirator, and occasionally it would suck in, his head moving with the effort, but that was all that moved. Julie had so many questions, but she just wanted to look at him. . .touch him. The nurse seemed to read her mind.

"You can touch him and let him know you're here. This is how you open these doors. Go on—he won't break. . .Dad, why don't you come around to the back here and hold his other hand? These little round doors operate the same way. . . I'll see if I can find the doctor to talk to you, unless you have some more questions I can answer right now. . . ?" Luke shook his head no, while Julie extended her hand into the incubator. She put one finger into little Luke's palm and her tears increased. The love and sorrow that flooded her whole being was bitter, sweet, strangling, and freeing all at once.

"Mommy's here, Luke," she whispered. "And Daddy. . . and Jesus. . .and we love you so much. . . ." Her trembling hand caressed his hair, still matted and sticky from his short stay in her womb. His skin was soft, delicate. She could see the blood vessels in his arms. He had the smallest fingernails she had ever seen; his tiny genitals declared his manhood, even as an infant of less than three pounds. *His little thighs are the meatiest thing on him,* she thought with a small smile. And his little feet reminded her of the pin depicting a pair of feet she wore on her winter coat, the symbol of the pro-life movement and the declaration of personhood for those even smaller than her Luke. She lovingly looked at his face—long eyelashes that he had inherited from the Schaeffer side of the family. His petite nose and cherubic mouth were half-covered with tape and had tubes protruding as ugly, distorting reminders that he shouldn't be out here yet—out where it was bright and noisy and cruel. She looked at her husband across the top of the incubator. He had one finger under Luke's left foot, but his eyes were on his wife.

"He is beautiful, isn't he, darling?" she asked, tears still blurring her vision.

"Told you," Luke smiled, "he's his mother's son."

"Mr. and Mrs. Vincent?" A swarthy man approached them and Luke stood to his full height, gently shutting the incubator porthole and extending his hand in return to the bearded man who spoke with an accent. "I'm Dr. Kute, one of the neonatologists. You met Dr. Barton earlier, but he's off duty now. First of all, congratulations."

They both mumbled a thank you. Julie kept her hand protectively over the body of her son. She wanted to hear what this stranger was going to say, but she didn't want to hear it either. She just wanted to hold young Luke and let Luke senior hold her. But she focused her attention on the doctor.

"Let me tell you where we stand. Right now your little boy is holding his own, but the next seventy-two hours are going to be rough. Normally, with no other complications, a baby Lucas's size would probably do fairly well. But the abruption has put him at some higher risk. It's too early to say anything definitive, but you need to know he's already demonstrated some seizure activity for which we're giving him some medication. He is early, as you know, and so all his organs are immature. He'll need the ventilator for a while, and we'll only be feeding him with IV fluids through those little catheters that go into his belly button. If one of us isn't around, the nurse can answer your questions. It's a lot of wait and see at this point, but we'll have some more answers as early as tomorrow. Do you have any questions I can answer?" He looked at both of them.

"Will he be brain-damaged?" Luke asked, hesitatingly. "I mean, are the seizures a real bad sign?" The physician thought a moment before answering.

"Well," he said, "they are not a good sign. Brain damage is a possibility and we want you to know that up front."

"We don't care, you know," Julie blurted out, her voice more harsh than she intended. "We. . .we want everything done for him."

"Everything will be done, Mrs. Vincent. We have a little time before we need to discuss those types of things." Julie didn't know what he meant exactly by "those types of things," but she didn't want to know and didn't ask. But she had to ask one question and her eyes pleaded with the doctor to give her the answer she wanted to hear.

"Will he make it? Is he going to live?" she asked, her finger and thumb gently grasping the hand of her newborn son. The doctor's hesitancy made her heart ache. It was worse than the white-hot pain of the abruption.

"We'll do our best," he said, "but it's too early to say."

"Dr. Burke or Barton or somebody said his chances are better than 80 percent," Luke interjected.

"Yes, that's true. But the abruption and the possibility that your baby has an infection complicates things. . .but, like I said, let's take it one step at a time for now and see how he does. He's been given antibiotics and some medicine to help his lungs, so we'll see how it goes. I don't want to give you a bleak picture or empty promises either, but a lot depends on Luke here. Anything else?"

What else could there be? Julie thought. *Please, God, she prayed, let him live. We don't care if he's brain-damaged or anything. Just let him live.* Luke thanked the doctor for them both and the nurse gave Luke some papers.

"These are visiting hours and such. Look all this over at your convenience. Parents and grandparents can visit anytime. We do have restrictions on other visitors, but you can read all that for yourselves. Can I answer any questions for you that Dr. Kute didn't cover?" she asked.

Julie tried again. "Do you think he'll live?" she asked.

The nurse seemed to understand her desperation and met Julie's eyes. "I hope so," she said, "but we just don't know yet. . .I'm sorry I can't give you a better answer. I know it's not one you want or need to hear," she said sympathetically.

"Will I be able to hold him?" Julie asked, knowing it was probably a stupid question. There were tubes and wires everywhere.

"Hopefully in a few days. It's a little early yet and these little guys get cold really fast outside their isolettes. As soon as we can do it, you'll be holding him. Maybe by the end of the week. Good enough?" she asked with a smile. Julie tried to smile back, but she wasn't very successful in her attempt.

"Good enough," she replied, stroking the head of the one who so quickly had captured her heart.

Julie returned to the present. To the empty nursery where there was no little Luke to demand her in the middle of the night or to coo over the bright mobile above the crib. The care had not been enough. Her prayers had not been enough. All their attempts to will life into their son had not been enough. It was not enough. And it was not good. Lucas Daniel Vincent had died when he was seventy-two hours old. She continued to rock. She was not crying. She hadn't cried —really cried—in weeks. She didn't think she had any tears left. She just ached inside.

She had rocked little Luke once. They had removed almost all the tubes and things and she and Luke had been able to be in a room alone with Lucas his last hour of life. They had talked to him, stroked him, prayed over him, and loved him. She had opened the little tee shirt they had placed on him and opened her blouse to lay him against her bare breast. She had wanted to know how it would feel to have him against her. Luke had held them both to him and wept. He hadn't cried since the day she had delivered. So they had rocked and wept together. They had even laughed a little bit.

They had never seen the back of their son: how his fine hair came to a long point at the base of his neck. He looked like a punk rocker. And his buttocks could hardly be called that: they were flat, shriveled, and devoid of any fat. They had caressed his long eyelashes and looked long at his tiny face, fixing it in their minds, wondering what it would have been like to see it grow and change and laugh. It had been a painful hour, but a wonderful hour. Just the three of them and Jesus.

Julie remembered how strongly she had sensed the Lord there with them. Even now she could close her eyes and almost see three people in the room. Three people weeping and smiling over Lucas. She had told her parents and Luke's about the ethereal calm that had pervaded the room that last hour. They too had let their children alone with their child. They had all said their good-byes before the life support was discontinued. The machine-free last hour had been reserved for Luke, Julie, and Lucas. And Jesus. That was how their families had prayed for them, and that was what had carried them through that day and the days that followed.

It was a long, dismal March. Even though Julie was ready physically to go back to school by April, she wasn't ready emotionally. The days she didn't cry just waking, she cried when she saw another baby, or even another little boy. She had taken the rest of the school year off.

Questions from well-meaning friends at church and relatives who called were all she could handle. She cried only intermittently now, but the loss was still real and always at the edge of consciousness, if not right in the middle of it. So she had arrived at September. She hadn't expected to return to teaching full-time after Luke's birth. Now her empty arms and the empty crib and the unpaid deductible of their hospitalization demanded her return to work. Childless, she would be facing a room full of children in less than a week. The next few days she would be facing other teachers and people from work, most of whom she hadn't seen since the memorial service. She bowed her head and stopped rocking.

"Help me, Lord. Help me through this day," was all she prayed.

"Julie! Welcome back!" Julie turned from her bulletin board to face the teachers who had classes across the hall from her. Both greeted her with warm hugs

"Hi, Lois, Megan. How are you two?" She stepped back and motioned for them to sit down. She took a final drink of her cup of coffee and sat down in one of the classroom chairs as they had. She hoped her smile didn't look as artificial as it felt.

"Fine."

"No complaints." Each answered simultaneously. An awkward silence ensued.

"Nice board, Julie," continued Megan. "I should have you come and give me a hand with mine. I have no flair for this sort of thing, you know. How you doing, Julie?" Megan hesitated. "Really." Her eyes were compassionate and her tone gentle.

"We're managing. I'm ready to get back into teaching again," she answered. "How are Bill and the kids? Did you guys go to Disney World like you had planned?"

"Yeah; it was great and the kids loved it. Lois and the boys were able to come too."

"The boys' dad and his new wife took a long vacation,

so it was nice Meg and Carl invited us along. This new change for them was hard. Alan hadn't been coming to pick them up as religiously as he was before he and his sweet young thing tied the knot, so it was good for them because of that too," Lois interjected bitterly. Julie remembered now that Lois and Alan's divorce had been final sometime around the time of Luke's death.

"You and Luke are doing okay?" Megan persisted. Julie appreciated Megan's consideration. She was probably her closest coworker.

"Well, some days are better than others, but we're doing all right," she answered.

"You're so thin, Juliette. Did you diet this summer to get rid of the weight you gained with the baby?" Lois asked. Megan gave Lois a withering look, but it was lost on Lois.

"Well, uh," Julie stumbled a little over her words. "No, I. . .I just haven't gained any weight lately—still not eating much, I guess."

"I lost a husband and didn't lose any weight," Lois shrugged. "Maybe if he'd died instead of divorced me I would have." Julie felt like she'd been slapped. She was at a loss for words, but Megan rescued her.

"Let's get back to work, Lois. I want to leave before three today, if I can." Megan almost yanked the smaller woman out of her chair. "We'll catch you later, Jules," she said to Julie, an apology in her eyes.

"Yeah. Come by our rooms tomorrow and give us a hand with our boards. And wait till you see that new male teacher. . ." Lois raised an eyebrow, but Megan propelled her out the door.

"I'll call you tonight," Megan said to Julie and they were gone. Julie sat in the chair stunned for a few minutes. She didn't know why Lois's comment had upset her, but she felt close to tears.

"So you came back!" A young woman of Julie's age came into the room, her long blond hair pulled back into a ponytail that reached almost to her waist. *This is not the time,* Julie thought, *for me to have to talk with our former Miss Pennsylvania.* The long-legged, attractive woman was never Miss Pennsylvania, but she almost had been and made sure everyone knew it. She sat at a table, her short skirt coming up to midthigh. Her blouse, *unbuttoned almost to her navel,* thought Julie, revealed a shimmering teddy underneath. As Julie recalled, Faye "Miss Pennsylvania" Nelson had had a few visits to the principal's office regarding her apparel. Julie recalled she had gotten better, but when the students weren't around, well, obviously Faye took advantage of their absence.

"I wasn't sure you'd be back this fall," Faye said, not unkindly. "How are you and that good-looking man of yours doing?"

"Luke and I are doing okay, thanks. How was your summer?" Julie stood again and continued working on her bulletin board. She felt unattractive and colorless next to the voluptuous Faye. She remembered asking Luke what he thought of Faye after she had introduced them at a Christmas party one of the other teachers had held.

"Well," he had muttered, suppressing a grin and scratching his ear. "She looks more like a beauty pageant debutante than a school teacher! I would have voted her 'Miss Pennsylvania' if her only talent was knowing how to walk without falling on her face." She was glad then and now that Faye worked with her and not with Luke. The word "piranha" often came unbidden to Julie's mind when Faye approached an attractive man.

"Wonderful!" she gushed, abruptly bringing Julie back to the present. "I moved out of Terry's apartment and dated several other men. There's a lot to that old proverb about variety being the spice of life." She cracked her gum and dangled a shoe from a perfectly pedicured toe. Julie noticed that Faye was "coordinated" from her nail polish to her lipstick. Even the trim on her camisole was the color of her fingertips and lips. Julie tried not to picture Faye getting dunked in a vat of mud, but it was hard.

"So, you're not seeing anyone special right now?" she asked.

"Oh, they're all special in one way or another," Faye purred. "But no, I'm not seeing just one guy right now. Have you met the new fifth-grade teacher yet?"

"Yes. Seems like a nice guy." *And probably your next victim,* Julie thought. *The poor guy is a marked man.*

"A very nice guy with some fine attributes," Faye concurred, interrupting Julie's thoughts again. Julie shook her head. She was thinking like a shrew. *Forgive me, Lord,* she prayed silently.

"So," continued Faye, "are you and the Programmer trying to make more babies? I thought you might try again since you lost the first one."

Julie kept working at her board, but her hand trembled and she tried to keep her voice from shaking. "No, I mean. . . uh. . .the doctor says I need to wait a while. . .give my body time to recover from the abruption and cesarean section." Using medical terms helped her somewhat; it made her loss less personal.

"Well, at least you can have more. I'd better get back to my room. If you need anything, you know where I am. Glad you're back." With that, Faye was out the door.

Julie sank into the nearest chair. She was close to tears and not sure she was ready for school after all. She closed her eyes and absently fondled the locket at her neck. She didn't care about other babies; she wanted her little Luke.

"Hello, Mrs. Vincent! How about lunch?"

Julie was startled and looked up to see her elderly neighbor peering in her doorway. She walked to the tiny woman who stepped into the room, a basket on her arm.

"Mrs. Day! Whatever are you doing here?"

"Lucas told me this was your first day back at school, so I decided to bring a lunch for the two of us to share." She looked around the room with a cluck of her tongue. "My, my. It hasn't changed much here. Such a nice board, Juliette! The children will like seeing their names there." She took Julie's hand. "Come along; let's go outside and enjoy this lunch."

They walked across the street to the small city park that boasted a well-cracked basketball court with no baskets hanging from the bent hoops. The grass, long overdue for mowing, was scraggly and full of weeds. The few swings that remained were in need of repair and the solitary picnic table was deeply etched with names, symbols, and graffiti. The mild early autumn temperature and bright sunshine made the park seem nicer than it was. Julie was glad for the diversion. Mrs. Day produced two tuna salad sandwiches, some sectioned apples, and a thermos of sugared, hot tea.

"This is delightful, Mrs. Day. What a kind thing for you to do!" Julie helped her spread their simple feast on the rough tabletop and poured their tea into two stained, hard plastic cups. She offered a prayer of thanks for the food— and secretly for Mrs. Day's visit—and the two sat in companionable silence for the first moments of their lunch.

"Is this your walk for the day?" Julie finally asked.

"Yes, it is. Don't know why I never thought of coming this way before. I usually go north on Parker and up and around the blocks towards the high school. Today I thought I'd try this and have lunch with you too. To be honest, it's always hard for me when you go back to school each fall. You spoil me all summer long with your visits and chauffeuring. And I'll tell you something else," she said with a wag of her finger. "These fancy running shoes are just the ticket. I should have invested in some a long time ago; I'm glad Lucas talked me into them."

Julie looked under the table at Mrs. Day's new shoes. She giggled with the discovery. Mrs. Day had on her usual polyester slacks, hose, and some white anklets. But there were her new high-top sneakers, daring anyone to call her old-fashioned.

"And you didn't forget your hot pepper spray, did you?" Julie asked.

"No, ma'am, I did not. This is America. The thugs out there don't know that I don't have anything that they want, but I'd have to spray them with this first to tell them so!" She brandished the protective spray that hung by a rubber band from her bony wrist.

Julie smiled at her neighbor. This was such a balm after the last hour at the school. She felt herself relaxing and sipped her tea. She almost never drank tea. When she did, she never put sugar in it. But she had learned to enjoy it that way with Mrs. Day.

"So, tell me how your day is going," Mrs. Day said.

"Okay. It's nice to see everyone again. We've got a couple of new teachers who seem like they'll fit in well. My class size isn't going to be too bad and the two worst kids in the sixth grade will be split up between Melinda Lowry and myself. At least neither of us got stuck with both of them."

"How else is your day going?" Mrs. Day asked quietly.

Julie's eyes met her neighbor's across the table. She told her elderly friend about Lois's remarks and the things Faye had said. She felt foolish as she struggled against crying again. She didn't sob, but the heaviness inside her demanded an outlet, and a few tears slid down her cheeks.

"She. . .talked about little Luke like he was some kind of replaceable commodity. I know she didn't mean it that way, but. . ." Words failed her and she dabbed at her eyes. "I remember reading in one of the booklets we got at the hospital to expect things like this. To expect people to say things they think offer comfort when they do just the opposite. But when you have it said right to your face, it's so devastating."

Mrs. Day nodded her head in agreement and reached across the table to pat Julie's hand. She took another sip of her tea and rubbed a spot on the side of her nose where the nosepiece of her glasses had left a deep cleft. She seemed to be thinking as she reseated her eyeglasses and patted Julie's hand again.

"Your friends, Juliette, do mean well. The one is hurting so much that she sees others' grief—including yours—through her own pain. The other one, she's young like you, isn't she?" Julie shook her head "yes."

"I thought so. She," continued Mrs. Day, "probably knows very little of suffering. Perhaps she has never known a terrible loss in her young life. She doesn't really know grief like you now know it. Life will teach her all about pain sooner or later. God can teach her how to live with it, how to manage day by day in spite of it. But she will not learn it from your pain. She can't. She's never been where you've been and she never will be either. Even if she herself one day loses a child, that child will not be little Luke. Only you and Luke lost Luke junior. His loss is unique to the two of you. I lost my son, Jeff, and I lost Harold. But I don't know what it was like to lose Luke any more than you know what it was like to lose Jeff or Harold. Yet," she hesitated before continuing and her gaze drifted away from Julie's face. "Yet," she repeated, "we each lost someone and we know a little of what it is like for the other, don't we?"

"Yes, we do," Julie answered quietly.

"I know you feel you have nothing to give now, but you do. You can give your friends time. Time to better sympathize with you. Time to know better what to say, or what not to say. Some of them may never be able to understand your loss. Perhaps they can't, or maybe they won't. It doesn't matter. You receive gratefully the intent that's there, and know that the Lord Jesus knows your pain, even in the midst of poor comforters. It may not seem like much sometimes, but it is enough. For each day, there is just enough."

The two women sat in silence again for a few moments. Julie drank the last of her tea and looked at her neighbor gratefully. "Thank you, Mrs. Day, for coming over. Thank you for your kind words."

"My, I certainly have gone on, haven't I? I had better let you get back to school." She began to gather the remains of their lunch. Julie wiped out their cups and tucked them into the basket.

"Why don't you and Luke join me for supper tonight? I'll make us a big pot of stew and some corn bread."

"You spoil us, Mrs. Day! I forgot to set out something for supper, so we'd be happy to come over. Can I bring salad or dessert?"

"No, no. I'll take care of everything. Why don't you bring the pictures you have of little Luke? I would like to see them again."

"Would you really?" Julie asked as they crossed the street. "You don't think it's being morbid?" Julie often looked at the pictures. She didn't think Luke had looked at them but once or twice in the months since little Luke's death. Looking at them helped her. She would touch the soft ringlet of hair the nurse had cut from the nape of little Luke's neck and gaze at his pictures, always amazed at the depth of her love for the child she knew for only a short time.

"No, I don't think it's being morbid. If Luke is uncomfortable about it, just bring them over some time soon when you and I can look at them. Sometimes men don't like to do things like that. You have to remember that young Luke's death is colored with the fact that Luke almost lost you too. His grief is different from yours because of that alone. Perhaps that wound is still too fresh for him to be able to enjoy the pictures of your son."

Julie had not thought of that before, even this morning when she recalled Luke's sobbing over her in the hospital. He had cried with her the day of the baby's death; he had cried at the funeral. Never had she seen him like he was at her bedside after the delivery: broken, sobbing, fear etched in his every feature. No wonder his constant concern over her health and return to work! Or his obsession with getting her to eat every bite of food at their meals! Even their lovemaking had been different since last winter. Luke was less spontaneous, always asking her if she was "up to it," and almost apologetic in his desire for her. He had always been an attentive, wonderful husband. Now that she thought about it, however, he seemed to be almost neurotic about her working too hard, or undertaking too many projects, or not getting enough sleep. And she had not seen any of it. Until today. She draped an arm across Mrs. Day's narrow shoulders.

"Thank you again for coming. Would 6:30 be too late?" They stopped at the front door of the school.

"No, that will be fine. See you tonight!"

Julie watched Mrs. Day's slow, steady trek up the street, her basket over one arm and clutched to her side. She turned once and waved, the hot pepper spray dangling from the rubber band at her wrist. *Mrs. Leona Day would have made you a wonderful third grandma, my dear son,* Julie thought. She pulled open the door and stepped back into the dull fluorescence of her school. Once inside, Julie thought of another way to brighten up her bulletin board. Her first day back at school was almost over, so she had better finish up soon.

She was eager to get home and show Luke he had not lost his wife too. She was very much alive and well! Together they would delight in the child they had had for a short time and in the life they still shared. They would mourn too, mourning that would always be with them. It would come often and sometimes at unexpected moments, but Julie was learning that this was the way of grief. Luke had been patiently, lovingly, perhaps often unknowingly, helping her through the painful days that had been. He was there for her. And she was here for him. God had spared her for her husband and so much more, she was certain.

She wiped a small tear from the corner of her eye and turned resolutely to the bulletin board. She had some final touches to complete. Her other children would soon be coming through her classroom door!

CHAPTER 10

First Impressions

R ubbish!"

Vic McCloskey pulled off his reading glasses to rub his eyes. He scrawled a C minus on the student's paper before him and leaned back, his desk chair making a squeaking protest against his push to relieve the taut muscles in his back. He threw down his red pen and turned off his study lamp. He had graded enough essays for the evening. Next time he would be sure to give a multiple-choice test. He was only three-quarters of the way through his English Literature 102 midterm papers. He knew if he graded any more to-night, he would probably flunk the whole lot of them.

He looked outside and a begrudging smile erased the scowl from his face. He was glad it was snowing again. He had all late classes tomorrow; he would get in a few hours of skiing in the morning before driving over to the college. He had lived in New York State all his life, but his move to up-state New York ten years ago when he took a position at Keaton College got him out of the big city. He still firmly believed it was the best move he had ever made. He turned his head side to side and stretched once more. His attention was caught by his Doberman, Ralph, who stood at his side, his leash in his mouth.

"Nobody would ever call you subtle, Ralph," he said, patting the dog on the head and taking the leash from him. "Let me get some clothes on and we'll go out for a bit." Vic walked to his bedroom and put on a flannel shirt and socks. In the summer he always sat around in shorts and sandals; in the winter it was jeans or shorts. He kept his house at a cool sixty-five degrees because he was perpetually warm. His brother was just the opposite: he wore layers of clothing all winter long and probably had never sweat a drop in his life. Vic seldom wore a heavy coat even in the coldest weather and had never had a blanket on his bed.

He admitted to being a born outdoorsman, but his outdoor interests were limited to skiing, hockey, and spectator football. Summers found him swimming and water skiing. All were sports suited to his chronic high body temperature and his "permanent fur coat," as his brother had always called it. Vic was a hairy man: his thick, auburn hair declared his Irish ancestry. He would probably never go bald, and if he did, his brother assured him that modern medicine could easily graft hair from any other part of his body to his head and no one would ever be able to tell the difference.

Vic smiled at the memory of a timeworn family joke. Their father had often referred to Vic and Vince as Esau and Jacob. The similarity between the two sets of brothers was limited to their physical appearances, however. Although Vince was more slender in his build than Vic, and didn't sport a five o'clock shadow by eleven in the morning like his brother did, he was the one who loved to hunt and fish. Vic left his musings and pulled on his socks and some walking shoes. He grabbed a light jacket from the hall closet. Ralph eagerly wagged his stump of a tail and danced around the front door, his paws clicking noisily on the terrazzo flooring.

"Okay, boy, let's take our stroll before it gets much later." Vic bent down to hook the leash onto Ralph's collar and they went out into the still night.

Big flakes rapidly accumulated on Vic's thick hair and bushy eyebrows. Ralph eagerly pulled at the leash, hastening Vic to a brisker walk. It was so cold that the snow was almost soundless beneath them. No wind blew and the January air felt good on Vic's face. He and Ralph were the only two out on the chill night and Vic relished the peaceful calm. He liked their small college town. Its population increased considerably during the school year, but the summers found very few students staying in Keaton. There weren't many summer jobs to be had. Vic enjoyed the pace here so much better than his years at Syracuse. Here he was able to get to know many of his students and he didn't have to teach twelve months of the year. He knew all of his colleagues, at least by name and face, and liked the small town atmosphere of Keaton. It wasn't a long drive to the nearest city of any size, and that was close enough for Vic. He and Ralph rounded the corner at the end of their block and proceeded up the main street that led into town. The Christmas decorations were still up and looked cheery, if somewhat out of date now, in the late January cold. Vic hesitated at the next street and decided to visit some friends he hadn't seen since the holidays. He tied Ralph's leash around the wrought-iron railing that circled the small concrete porch.

Vic had met Dave and Milly Fenton soon after moving to Keaton. Vic had many friends who were married couples, but his friendship with the Fentons was unique. Vic never felt awkward with Dave and Milly and their children. He had often watched David and Amy for Dave and Milly and he felt no different being with them than with his brother and his family. Unfortunately, Milly was an incorrigible matchmaker. Especially where Vic was concerned. He rang the doorbell.

"Victor McCloskey! It's about time you paid us a visit!" She hugged him to her and pulled him in at the same time. "Hello, Ralph! One of the kids will bring you a treat," she promised the dog, who was already noisily sniffing around the snow-covered flower beds.

"Amy! David! Uncle Vic is here!" she called. An almost-teenaged boy and his nine-year-old sister came down the stairs to greet their "adopted uncle." Amy still gave Vic a hug when she saw him, but David was outgrowing such affectionate displays. He smiled warmly at Vic and laughed when Vic feigned a punch to his stomach and then took him down to the family room in a bear hug. He pinned David to the floor with his massive bulk and shook snow from his head onto David's laughing face.

"Mercy!" David yelled between his laughter and gasps for air. "You're smashing me, Uncle Vic! I can't breathe. . . !"

Vic let up and fast as a cat David was on his back,

attempting to wrestle Vic from his knees to a more vulnerable prone position. Amy joined her brother in the fray and both of them managed to be sitting on Vic's chest and stomach in short order—mostly due to Amy tickling Vic's neck, which made him weak with laughter. Milly sat resigned in the chair, shaking her head.

"Don't the three of you ever tire of this?" she asked, only to be ignored. The melee continued for a few more minutes before she called an end to it. "Okay, you two. I know Vic started it, but you've got homework to finish." Vic took his cue and pulled himself up after doing some tickling himself and threw both children lightly off him with little effort.

"You heard your mom, monsters," he added, wiping his brow and standing to his feet. "Besides, Ralph—"

"Ralph's here?" they both exclaimed simultaneously. They started for the door, but their mother's command stopped them.

"Coats, my children—and hats. And gloves. Then you can join the other rabble-rouser. Walk him just down to Baxters' before you give him any biscuits. Don't be gone long; the homework waits."

Vic dropped onto the sofa with a sigh, smoothing his now wild-looking hair. His blue eyes twinkled and his cheeks were red from the horseplay. "I needed some exercise," he said. "I know I can always get it from the kids."

"Well," Milly handed him a cup of coffee she had brought in during the altercation, "the kids need to get their homework done, too. Next time you visit on a school night a simple 'hi' will suffice." She smiled her rebuke and sat back down next to Vic.

"Where's David senior?" he asked.

"He's working afternoons this week. It's nice to have him with me every night, but the kids don't see much of him. We'll be glad when he's back on midnights again next week. We haven't seen you since Christmas, Vic. What have you been doing? Skiing every free day you've got?"

"Not quite. I'm teaching an extra course this quarter, so it's taking up a little more time. I'm back in my discipleship group too with those three young guys I was meeting with before the holidays, so I've kept busy."

"No one else special in your life?" Milly asked with raised eyebrows.

Vic shook his head and took a long drink of his coffee. "You never give up, do you, Mil? The perpetual matchmaker. . ."

"Mom," David stopped at the door before going out. "Are you bothering Uncle Vic again?" Amy giggled behind her brother.

"If you two are going, you'd better go now," their mother returned, not answering her son's question. The two children went outside, Ralph's excited barks and their greetings to him suddenly muffled by the door's closing.

"Is my love life the subject of the entire family?" Vic asked good-humoredly.

"You mean your lack of a love life?" Milly replied, setting her mug down. She turned to face Vic and he recognized the familiar stance.

"I know that look, Mildred," he said as he walked to the kitchen. "Just forget it. The last woman you lined up for me had a voice that made my hair stand on end and the one before that weighed more than me." He returned to the sofa, stirring his refilled cup of coffee.

"Now, Vic, you're too nice of a guy to let go to waste."

" 'Waste!' I have a good job, a nice house, a loyal dog, enough outside interests to keep me entertained and challenged—"

"But you need someone to share it with," Milly interrupted, her mouth down in a pout.

"Listen, Mil—" he started.

"No, you listen, Vic." Milly pulled both her legs up under her onto the couch and her face became as animated as her voice. This was also a stance Vic recognized. He started to get up, but she grabbed his arm. "This one is a winner," she said confidently. "You've got to meet her."

Vic groaned. "I'm always meeting these 'winners' you line up for me, Milly. Give a man a rest, would you?" He leaned his head back and closed his eyes.

"Even Dave approves of this one, Vic," she coaxed. "Let me tell you about her."

"Oh, Mil—"

"No, hear me out. She's a lot like you, Vic: tall, hair about your color, an avid skier, thirty-something, and available."

"Which, translated, means she's big, hairy, will take me out on the slopes, and is an old maid. Don't you weary of this, Milly?" he asked with some feigned, and some genuine, exasperation.

"I've told you I've made it my goal to get a wife for you and some 'cousins' for the kids. Let's make some plans for you to meet her."

"Let's not. I'm too busy right now. Maybe spring break. Can I borrow that fancy serving dish of yours again to take a cake to our Sunday school class party next week?" he asked.

"Yes, but don't change the subject. How about the four of us doing a dinner and movie. . . ?"

"No, Milly. Maybe some other time. Hey! You're back!" Vic got up from the couch and went to the door where Amy and David stood, stomping off their snowy boots on the small throw rug.

Milly got up and took the children's coats from them. "This discussion is not closed," she said quietly out of the side of her mouth to Vic.

"It never is," he answered with a wry smile. He pulled his own jacket back on and tousled David's hair. "Tell Dave to give me a call over the weekend. I'll get that serving dish from you Saturday. See you, Mil; see ya, kids," he said and stepped out the door.

Milly stood at the door, holding it propped open with her foot. "Why don't you come by Friday for supper? Dave's off and you can get it then. Six o'clock okay?"

"Sure—but no surprises, Milly." He patted Ralph's head and started down the walk.

" Bye, Vic!" she called, but then muttered to herself, "Just one surprise, dear old Uncle Vic." She smiled and closed the door.

Thursday morning arrived with radiant sunlight that made the six inches of fresh snow sparkle with a blinding intensity. The temperature was well below the freezing mark and Vic felt small beads of perspiration across his forehead as he came down his favorite run of moguls as fast as he could, expertly jumping and bouncing from mound to mound, the powdery snow a brilliant cloud of white around and behind him. The last portion of the run he skied easily to the chairlift, somewhat winded and glad he had decided to come before his day's classes. He exchanged pleasantries with the lift attendant and then rode up with a man twice his age from Ontario who said he was "making the rounds of the USA's Midwest ski resorts." They parted company at the top and Vic skied towards one of the long, meandering trails to finish his invigorating morning before going to the school.

Vic was admiring the scenery around him when he thought he heard a panic-stricken scream behind him. He turned slightly just as another skier slammed into him, her head banging into his cheekbone just below his goggles. Her skis went over his, one leg between his legs, and Vic felt himself falling forward. His goggles flew off his face, he felt one ski break loose, and in the same second he was tumbling in the powder, keeping his body loose to roll with his induced fall. It was only a matter of seconds when he stopped and could take a full assessment of the situation. He was fine— just without goggles, which he presumed were somewhere near. He still had one ski on, which he popped off and parked in the snow next to his now one and one-half ski poles. He quickly made his way five or six feet up the rise of the hill to the groaning lump of humanity that lay sprawled under the snow. Her skis were off, her poles gone, and her hat further up the hill next to one of her skis.

"Are you all right?" Vic reached for the woman, but did not move her. He peered around at her face. "Can you hear me?"

She just groaned and hardly lifted her face out of the snow. "Please, God," he heard her say, "let me be dead." She raised her head and looked at her victim through snow-frosted eyelashes. Her pale green eyes were apologetic.

"I am so sorry," she said with a heavy southern accent. She rolled over with a groan and sat in the snow, brushing off her jacket and deep auburn hair. "Did I hurt you?" she asked Vic. Her hand went to her mouth and she gasped. "Oh, your face!"

"Are you okay?" A fellow skier slowed, bringing some of their equipment to them.

"Yeah, fine. Thanks." Vic took the woman's skis from the man and stuck them in the snow. Their Good Samaritan went on his way and Vic turned back to his accidental assailant.

"Can you get up?" he asked, offering his hand. She took it and stood somewhat clumsily to her feet. Her eyes widened.

"Did. . .did I do that to your face?" she asked. She removed a glove and reached up to touch Vic's cheek. He winced and jerked his head back at the sudden pain. He took off his gloves and felt a swelling below his eye.

"I'll live. No worse than anything else I've had before. Let's get you back down the hill and then I can get some ice on my face. Sure you're okay?" he asked again. He saw her make a face and look down the remaining slope of the run. He reached down to grab some snow and put it on the rapidly swelling area over his right cheekbone.

"Is there another way down?" she asked.

Vic continued to gather equipment and rested his goggles around his neck. " 'Fraid not," he said. "Unless you want to try to walk down. It's not too steep the rest of the way."

"I'll walk," she said. "I'm shakin' too much to try any more skiin' today." She balanced her skies on a shoulder and tucked her poles under her arm.

"I'll help you ski down," Vic volunteered, secretly hoping to hear more of her smooth southern drawl.

"Not a chance. I'm gonna find that ski instructor of mine and take another lesson after a big glass of hot cocoa. I am sorry again, sir," she said, and started down the hill. Vic snapped on his skis and kept his poles in his hand.

"Let me carry your skis and poles down for you. I'll put them to the right of the lodge."

She seemed to think about it for a moment and then consented. "I am in your debt, sir," she said, and handed him her equipment without another word.

"Are you sure. . . ?" he started before heading down the hill.

"Very. Thank you."

Vic looked back up the hill once to see the woman slowly coming down the hill—sometimes walking, sometimes tripping. He shook his head and parked her equipment at the north end of the building. He removed his own skis and went inside. He could see her still struggling down the hill; she was still snowy and had left her goggles hanging around her neck. She looked no more graceful off the skis than she had been on them. Vic walked to the restroom to assess the damage to his face. His reflection in the mirror told him he was going to have a black-and-blue face for a while and probably a shiner to go with it. He went to get some ice.

"What happened to you, Vic?" the woman behind the counter asked. "The moguls or trees get the better of you today?" She handed him his requested bag of ice and a cup of coffee.

"No, another skier got the best of me. Can't you guys put up a sign that says, No Novices Allowed? It would make it a lot safer for the rest of us."

"And lose half our business? Not a chance! At least you didn't break the skin." She rang up the cash register and returned his change.

"No, just one of my poles. See you later, Shirley. I've got to get over to the school." Vic went to retrieve his equipment. He would have to hurry to get showered and shaved before his one o'clock class.

It was late Thursday night when Vic and his Bible study group broke for the evening. Charlie and Ed had left for the night; Todd had remained a little longer to talk with Vic privately. He slumped in the chair where he sat. The lines of worry etched on his forehead and around his mouth made him appear much older than his twenty years. The three young men that Vic met with every week were an odd mix: Charlie, an athlete and popular young man on campus; Ed, a single-minded young man who did little else than study; and Todd, a man who was neither popular nor focused. He had the sensitivity of a child and struggled in a world unfriendly to his childlike heart.

"So your visit home at Christmas wasn't a very good one, Todd?" Vic asked.

"No worse or better than usual, I suppose," Todd answered. Vic waited for him to continue. "My brother got plastered New Year's and he and Dad just about came to blows. Phil doesn't like Dad's new girlfriend—or maybe he does like her, but not as a potential stepmother. Anyway, I ended up being the arbitrator like always. But it was ugly and just. . ." He searched for the right words. "Well, it just wasn't very nice to be home. Mom's been dead for over two years now, but her being gone seemed harder this year than last. I guess it's because of the way Dad is. He's like a different man: obnoxious, loud, vulgar. . .I hardly know him anymore! It's like I lost both my parents when Mom died, only some alien moved into my dad's body." He looked down at his ragged, bitten fingernails. He raised his eyes to Vic again and smiled the sad smile Vic had grown accustomed to seeing. "I've been watching too much science fiction," he said.

Vic smiled in sympathy. "I know you've said before what a difficult thing your mother's death was for your family. Your dad took care of her a lot her last few months of life, didn't he?"

"Yeah. We had hospice in the last week or so, but Dad

did take a lot of time off work to care for Mom. The girls did essentially all the homey things: laundry, meals, and all that. But Dad cared for Mom: fed her, bathed her, read to her. . . He used up all his vacation time at work just to have more time with her. That's why his personality change is so hard to take. I mean, now he's like he used to be when we kids were growing up. I'd gotten used to the somber man he had become during Mom's last year and the year after her death. So, maybe the alien was the guy who was around a couple of years and the real Dad is back." He looked blankly at the fire going in the fireplace. Vic remained silent, letting him talk.

"This new girlfriend is something else. She's too young for Dad, for one thing. She tries too hard to please all of us and is embarrassed when her two kids start arguing over toys or whatever. It was a very uncomfortable holiday, that's for sure. Did I tell you her name?" Vic shook his head as Todd continued. "Ginger. Is that a name or what?" Todd stood and reached for his coat.

"I gotta get going, Vic. Thanks for listening to my rambling." He pulled on his coat and picked up his Bible and notepad. Vic walked him to the door.

"I'll see you next week, Todd. Give me a call if you need anything. Don't judge your dad too harshly. Just keep being there for him—even if you're just a referee sometimes. Give him more time. He spent more than half his life with your mother. He's probably still trying to learn just who he is without her. We all heal at different speeds."

Todd gave him a lopsided grin. "You'd better hope you're a fast healer. You are a sorry sight with that face and eye of yours. See ya, Vic."

"Good night." Vic closed the door after him and brought his hand up to the right side of his face. The swelling had subsided somewhat, but the bruising was a bold purple and red. The white of his right eye was a bright crimson. It didn't hurt much, but it looked bad. He turned out the lights and sat again in his study to watch the fire and pray before retiring.

Each visit home for Todd seemed to make him more morose. He had not been a Christian for long and the difficulties of his home situation seemed to stress him unduly. Vic suspected there were more problems in Todd's relationship with his father than these more recent ones, but he was not one to push someone into sharing deeply private matters—especially if they were unpleasant ones. He would continue to listen and advise when it seemed appropriate. Mostly he would continue to pray for Todd. Vic didn't feel well-equipped to deal with the emotional maelstrom that he sensed in Todd, but he wanted to help him if he could. He bowed his head for what would be a long hour of prayer for his young friend.

After his classes on Friday, Vic took Ralph to the park before going over to Dave and Milly's. It was snowing again and he pulled on his hiking boots, coat, and gloves. It had been windy all day and the temperature was below zero. By the time he had arrived at the house, he wished he had put on a hat; even he was cold in the subzero temperature.

"Come on in, Vic," Dave opened the door for him and took his coat once he was inside. "It will just be the four of us tonight. Davey is at a party at church and Amy's at the neighbor's staying with a friend. The girls are still working on supper. Can you give me a—hey! What happened to your face, man?" Dave had gotten a better look at Vic once he was inside.

"Some novice skier blindsided me yesterday. What's this about the 'four of us'?" Vic asked. Dave motioned for him to follow him upstairs.

"Milly didn't tell you?"

"Tell me what?" Vic followed his friend into Amy's bedroom.

"Help me move this dresser, would you? Milly's decided Amy's room has to be painted tomorrow." The two men moved it easily and Dave pointed to the bed. "This will just roll out easily. She didn't tell you about Lucy?" Dave grunted as they pushed the bed away from the wall. Vic stood up and crossed his arms across his chest.

"Lucy who? Would you finish one topic before moving on to another? You're starting to talk like your wife!" Vic looked at Dave with a roll of his eyes as the realization of what was about to take place registered. "Not again," he groaned.

"You'll like this one, Vic. She's almost as good-looking as Milly and has a southern drawl that will knock your socks off." Dave started to propel Vic back towards the steps, but Vic stopped suddenly, almost making Dave run into him.

"Don't tell me—she's got freckles and went skiing Thursday."

"Freckles? Now that you mention it, yeah, I think she does." Dave continued down the stairs to the kitchen. "I don't know about the skiing part, but—" He stopped on the stairs and it was Vic's turn to almost run into Dave. Dave lowered his voice. "Try to act the part of the courteous college professor, would you? Not the lout we know is the real you."

"Why do you let your wife do this to me, Dave? Can't you keep her under better control?" Vic whispered. They could hear the women's voices as they came closer to the kitchen.

"And miss all this fun? Not on your life!" Dave walked into the kitchen with more enthusiasm than Vic. "We're ready to eat, ladies!" he announced, picking a piece of lettuce out of the salad bowl and popping it in his mouth.

Milly and her companion turned towards them. In one glance Vic noticed Milly's shocked look when she saw his face and the other woman's hand go to her mouth, her light green eyes showing recognition.

"Vic McCloskey! What happened to your face?" Milly came towards him with her mothering look and Vic backed away, holding up his hands in readied defense.

"I'm fine, Milly. Just a mishap on the slopes."

A brief, awkward silence followed. Dave looked at Vic with a questioning face.

"Have you and Lucy met?"

"This is so embarrassin'," Vic heard Lucy mumble, but then she raised her head again and smiled weakly. "In a manner of speakin', yes, David, your friend, Vic, and I have met." She held out her bandaged hand to Vic, who took it ever so gently and shook it. "I am so sorry again, Mr. McCloskey." She followed his gaze to her hand and shook her head. "Yes, I did this Thursday too—took a few stitches after runnin' over my instructor and landin' in a tree." Vic tried not to smile, but lowered his head briefly and covered his amusement with a cough.

"So you two know each other?" Milly asked, setting down the spoon she was holding and pulling Vic to the table and sitting him in a chair. "Let me look at that eye—"

Vic brushed her away. "I'm fine, Milly. You tend to your stew there."

"You guys met Thurs—are you the one who gave Vic the shiner?" Dave asked with a dawning laugh.

"I thought you ran into another woman, Lucy." Milly returned to her oven to check the biscuits.

"I ran into a lot of people that day, Milly," she confessed, her face still a blush.

Vic noticed a small scar at her throat since the whiteness of it contrasted boldly with the pink of her neck, face, and ears. Her short, curly hair was considerably more under control than it had been at the ski resort two days ago. She had lightly penciled her eyebrows and was wearing black mascara on her eyelashes. He didn't like a lot of makeup and thought she had looked better Thursday with snow on her eyelashes and wet ringlets around her face. He shook off the thought. He would get through this evening and quickly exit Miss Lucy's life. It would be much safer.

"I'm Lucy Evers, Mr.—"

Milly cut her off. "I'm so sorry, Lucy. We're forgetting our manners," Milly interjected.

"No need for formal introductions or formality, ladies.

Please, call me Vic," he said quickly to Lucy. "I assume you just moved here. Your accent suggests the South."

"Yes. Moved up here from Tennessee. I have some friends and family who live in Lake Placid, but I got a job here in Keaton and it's not much of a drive there. Let me help you, Milly." She turned back to her hostess.

The women set the table and after grace was offered, the four of them conversed fairly easily through the meal. Vic had learned how to avoid Milly's secret smiles and raised eyebrows that always said, "What do you think?" or "Wouldn't she make a nice wife?" Instead he concentrated on everyone else and the food. He didn't miss Dave frequently grinning as he took a sip of water and wondered if their ill-concealed mirth was as obvious to Lucy as it was to him. He hated this matchmaking stuff, but tried to be courteous since he knew Lucy was as innocent a victim as he was and that Milly meant well.

Dave always found these arranged events of Milly's entertaining. Often they went well, occasionally they were disastrous, but mostly they were unpredictable and Dave liked that best of all. He and Vic had talked about it on occasion. Dave was always amused and not very sympathetic. Vic always grumbled and promised himself he wouldn't let Milly talk, cajole, or manipulate him into another introduction to a member of the opposite sex.

"How did you meet Milly, Lucy?" Vic asked as they started to gather up the dishes after supper.

"At an aerobics class. I needed some exercise—it is so cold here that there's not much else to do to keep warm!"

"You're still doing that aerobics stuff, Mil? Why don't you get out and take some skiing lessons with Lucy?" Vic handed her the stack of empty salad bowls.

"And get all banged up like you two? Not a chance! Listen, you can't help with these dishes with your hand, Lucy. Why don't you and Vic get stuff set up in the family room for some cards or something? Vic, you know where everything is. Dave can help me load the dishwasher. It will only take us a minute."

While Vic pulled the chairs and card table out of the closet, Lucy looked up at the pictures on the fireplace mantle.

"This is a good picture of the children," she said. "Is the dog with them theirs?"

Vic wiped his brow and pulled off his sweatshirt. He was getting warmer by the minute. He should have known better than to dress so warmly. He sat down in Dave's favorite chair. He didn't know how Dave did it, living in a house that was as warm as an oven.

"No," he said, answering Lucy's question. "It's my dog, Ralph. He and the kids are best friends." He noticed Lucy shiver and she rubbed her arms.

"Are you cold, Lucy?" he asked. "I could stoke the fire more."

"No, I'll be all right, thanks."

An awkward silence followed and Vic could hear Milly and Dave talking quietly in the kitchen. He was afraid he'd fall asleep sitting in Dave's favorite chair. The comfort of the chair and the temperature of the room were making him sleepy. He shook his head and ran his hand through his thick hair. He struggled to keep the conversation going.

"Do you have any other interests outside of aerobics and learning how to downhill, Lucy?" He watched her curl one tendril of hair about a finger. Her hair was the same color as his, as Milly had said. Lucy was tall too; he would guess just a few inches shorter than his own six-foot-two frame.

"Not many," she replied. "I'm an avid swimmer and I sing and play the guitar, but that's about all. I'd like to learn some activities I can enjoy here in New York. I don't know if skiin's gonna be one of them," she said with a small smile and a shake of her head. "Excuse me a minute, Vic," she said and left the room.

Vic yawned and allowed himself the luxury of closing his eyes for what he was sure was only a minute or two.

"Victor McCloskey!" Milly's whispered scolding and slap on his knee roused him abruptly. "Did you frighten Lucy off with your snoring?"

"I wasn't snoring. She just went into the bathroom." Vic stood and stretched again. Lucy came back and sat in the chair closest to the fireplace.

"Let me get you a sweater, Lucy. I keep forgetting about how cold you always are." Milly left the room for a minute while Dave and Vic both sat down. Vic thought it was curious she had refused his offer to stoke the fire, but he shrugged it off without a second thought.

"Thank you, Milly. What are we going to play?" she asked.

Milly brought an assortment of games and cards to the table. It was after ten minutes of arguing and banter that they decided on Scrabble. The men were pitted against the women and the game went until almost midnight. It was the women who won; Lucy's last word "fetlock," which they had to look up to verify, won the game.

"You have to remember that I come from Tennessee—and from that part of Tennessee near Kentucky," Lucy smiled. "I know a lot about horses."

"More than any of us, that's for sure!" Dave laughed. He and Vic gathered up the table and chairs.

"Anyone for some decaf?" Milly asked.

"No," Vic and Lucy answered simultaneously. Vic continued. "I need to get home, Milly, thanks. I have to get that dish from you, too."

"I almost forgot. Come with me into the kitchen. I don't think I can reach it without a chair and you'll probably be able to get it." Vic followed Milly into the kitchen and left Dave talking with Lucy as he got her coat.

"So?" Milly whispered to Vic as he reached for the dish. "What do you think of her? Isn't she absolutely 'charmin'?" she asked, putting a slow drawl to her last word.

"Yes, Mil. She's a nice lady."

"And attractive?" Milly persisted. Vic thought of the black mascara and penciled eyebrows, but decided to avoid a rabid defense of the woman from Milly.

"Yes, she's attractive, Milly. I'll bring this back next week." He hurried out of the kitchen before she could say more. Lucy was apologizing to Dave as they entered the living room.

"It was so clumsy of me, Dave. . . ." Lucy was picking

up ice cubes and a glass from the carpet.

"Don't worry about it, Lucy—it was just ice. The kids track in so much snow and dirt that this is nothing. Go on; we'll take care of it." He took the glass from her and set it on the end table.

"Thanks for the evening, Mil. . .Dave." Vic pulled on his coat. "And for the meal; it was great. It was nice meeting you, Lucy. Be careful on the slopes."

"I plan to stay far away from them for a while," she smiled. They all shared a final good-bye and Lucy and Vic left. Vic started down the walk as Lucy turned towards her car. He sensed her hesitate and then heard her sigh.

"It's terribly cold, Vic. Can I give you a lift?"

"No, I'm fine, thanks. The walk will do me good. Good night, Lucy."

Vic walked briskly towards his house. It was still bitterly cold, but it felt good this time after being so hot at Dave's. He waved back at Lucy who almost hit the stop sign at the corner when she waved a final time at him. "Glad I walked," he mumbled to himself. He watched the taillights of her car disappear down the road. He had successfully endured another of Milly's schemed blind dates. The ball was in his court now. He planned to leave the court and let the ball remain there.

Vic's next two weeks were full with classes, filling in for another professor, and meeting with his small group of young men. He hadn't thought of Lucy Evers since that night at Dave and Milly's. Well. . .he had thought of her once or twice, maybe, but only briefly. He had to admit he liked listening to her talk, but when he remembered the eyebrows he shook his head and quickly forgot about her.

It was a Monday evening the next time Vic saw, or rather, heard Lucy Evers. He and Charlie were having a cup of coffee and some dessert at a local restaurant. Charlie had gotten up to answer his pocket pager when Vic heard the voices behind him. He was sure it was Lucy; there was little mistaking her voice. He was about to say hello when her words stopped him.

"This friend of mine arranged for me to meet a friend of hers and her husband's a few weeks ago. . . ." He smiled when he heard the inflection at the end of her sentence. It sounded like she was asking a question instead of making a statement.

"This guy," she continued, "looked like a bear who had just come out of hibernatin'!" He heard her companion giggle. "I mean," she went on, "he was this big monster with more hair than a grizzly and who perspired—I mean, honey, he dripped! Constantly! The whole evenin'! He was nice, I suppose, but he was such a stuffed shirt talkin' about his college, and his students, and his dog, and his. . .well, you know what I mean. He acted like I should be flattered just to be in the same room with him! Insufferable—that's what he was."

Vic sat stunned. Had he given that impression? He thought he had been as charming as Cinderella's prince!

"Anyway, my friend, she says, 'You just have to get to know him better, Lucy. He's just a little shy at first.' I told her I know the difference between 'shy' and just plain ole stuck-up. She hasn't bothered me about him since."

Milly hadn't pestered him about calling Lucy; now Vic knew why. He scratched his unruly hair and shook his head. Had he really acted like that? As for sweating, well, what did she expect when someone kept his house like an oven? Lucy had begun another tirade when Charlie returned to the booth. Vic heard the clink of dishes and Lucy apologize; she must have knocked over something on the table.

"Sorry, Vic. I had to talk a guy through a computer problem over at the office. This part-time job is good money, but this on-call stuff is starting to weary me a bit. Ready to go?"

"Let me finish this cup of coffee first." Vic hoped Lucy and her friend would leave before them. He didn't want to embarrass her again when she realized he was sitting behind her, possibly hearing everything she said. He didn't want to face her either, knowing now what he knew.

Vic had to stay at the restaurant longer than he had wanted to since he waited until Lucy left. He tried to shrug off what he had heard, but it bothered him somewhat—both that she found him rude and unattractive. He knew he was no prize, but he had always thought women regarded him as, well, ruggedly handsome in his own way. He had been sorely mistaken, obviously. After dropping Charlie off at his dorm, Vic drove over to the building that housed his office. He was noisily going through his keys when he noticed his office door ajar. The cleaning lady's cart was parked in the hallway. He heard a low, mellow alto voice as he went in. He called out so as not to startle the woman.

"Hello! It's only Dr. McCloskey, Gertie." He stopped when he wasn't facing Gertie. It was Lucy Evers, complete in an old sweat suit and with most of her makeup worn off. She blushed slightly then waved her dust rag.

"Come in, professor," she said, her voice implying she didn't think him worthy of the title. "I just finished."

He set down his briefcase and pulled his cap from his head. "I didn't know you worked for the college, Lucy. Where is Gertie?"

"I work here part-time on her nights off. It supplements what little I make at the telephone company. It's expensive livin' up here." She set down the telephone after dusting under it. "Well, good night. You'll lock up when you leave?" She went out the door without waiting for an answer. Vic put his briefcase on his desk and followed her out the door. He was determined she not continue to think him the conceited oaf he had apparently caused her to think he was.

"Uh, Lucy. . ."

"Yes?" She turned her light green eyes on him question-ingly. Vic thought she looked ready for a fight.

"Uh. . ." he repeated, "done any more skiing?"

"No. I just had the stitches out of my hand a few days back," her voice lifted like a question.

Vic ran his hand through his hair. "Oh, yes. How is it?"

"It's fine," she replied. Vic was about to ask her another question in an attempt to make some light conversation, but she spoke before he did.

"Listen, Vic. I've got work to do. Is there anything else?" She put one hand on the cart and the other on her hip, *almost daring me to take up any more of her time,* he thought.

"No. . .nice to see you ag—"

"Good night, professor." She gave him a patronizing smile and her cart a push. The cart hit his foot with a "thunk" and Vic winced as it rolled onto one of his bunions. Lucy's bored expression left her face immediately as she came around the cart, apologizing profusely.

"I'm so sorry, Vic. Are you all right?"

He hobbled back to his desk chair and pulled off his shoe to rub his foot. He held out his hand to keep Lucy away from him. "I'm fine," he said through clenched teeth. The woman was a menace, he decided, and subliminally (or otherwise) was out to remove his huge, hairy frame from the earth.

"I'm okay. Just got a bunion that doesn't take kindly to being run over." He rubbed his foot a few more seconds and put his shoe back on. He looked up at her and the cool indifference was gone. He thought about saying something like: Can we start over again? But changed his mind. "I won't keep you from your work, Lucy. Good night."

" 'Night," she said and left his office for the next one.

Vic tied his shoelace and pulled some papers out of his briefcase. He shook his head and put the books he had come for in his briefcase. He heard Lucy singing a tune he didn't know. He listened a few more minutes before leaving. *She can't ski and she doesn't clean very well,* he thought, rubbing his hand along the edge of his file cabinet and finding it still dusty. He frowned at the dust and wiped his hand on his jeans. She could sing, however. He locked his office and left for the night. The lady could sing.

The next day Vic sat at his desk at home drumming his fingers on the book opened before him. He was not studying, but trying to decide if he should call Lucy. He wasn't interested in her romantically, but it still bothered him that he had made such a bad impression. The ringing of his telephone interrupted his musings. He had barely said "hello" when Milly jumped to the subject at hand.

"Busy tonight, Victor?" she asked. "Lucy is going to be doing a miniconcert at her church and I thought you would like to go with Dave, the kids, and me."

"I don't think so, Mil. Lucy didn't exactly take to me, you know, and she's not my—"

"Oh, fiddle-faddle, Vic," she cut in.

"Fiddle-faddle? Where on earth did you dig up that old expression?"

"My great-grandma. What do you say? We could pick you up at 6:30."

"No, Mil. I don't think it's a good idea." Vic closed his book and laid his glasses down.

"Come on, Vic. You need to get out more. Besides, you and Lucy are perfect for each other. You just don't know it yet." He heard her say something to one of the kids before he answered.

"Listen, Milly. Lucy does not like me. I ran into her over at the school and she made that very clear."

"Lucy doesn't know what she likes. We'll be by to pick you up."

"No, you won't."

At 6:50 Vic found himself climbing out of the Fentons' van, giving Dave a hopeless shake of his head. He hadn't told either of them what he had overheard in the restaurant, but had them laughing when he told them how Lucy had tried to run him down with her cleaning cart. He was still mumbling to himself when they sat down in the little storefront church.

"Stop grousing, Vic," Milly whispered around Dave. "We're here for a concert—not your wedding."

The service was unlike any Vic had previously attended. The music was spirited and there was a lot of hand-clapping and spontaneous "hallelujahs" and "yes, Lord," and a few other words he didn't understand. A long period of praying, praise, and what he secretly dubbed "wailing" followed the singing and then more singing broke out. He looked at his watch and wondered how long the evening would be. This free-spirited praise was not his style and he wasn't sure if he liked it or not. Amy's eyes were big and young Dave rolled his eyes at Vic several times. Vic stole a few furtive glances at Dave and Milly, but Dave had his hands up, his eyes closed, and a smile on his face. Milly too was smiling, but vocal with some "amens" and avid hand-clapping. Vic wondered if he and the kids were the only ones in the whole place who still had their wits about them.

Finally everyone sat down and someone whom Vic assumed was the pastor stood up and introduced Lucy. Lucy sat on a high stool and briefly fine-tuned her guitar. She smiled at her small audience and began singing and playing

"Turn Your Eyes Upon Jesus."

The entire atmosphere of the room changed. It had been noisy, happy, and unrestrained; now solemnity, quiet anticipation, and an almost palpable reverence permeated the room like a delicate, sweet aroma. Lucy never talked; she simply sang or played a melodic pathway from one song to another. Vic felt himself being transported away from the building, from Dave and Milly, from the kids, and even from Lucy. The songs and music sang. . .Jesus. One minute Vic would be silently praying as images of people came to his mind. The next he would be praising God, acutely aware of the beauty and power of Jesus Christ. The words of "Embrace the Cross" fired his imagination and soul with horror, love, and a host of other incongruous feelings and thoughts. It was sobering and exultant all at once. Lucy's last song brought him slowly, gently back to the room in which they all sat. Vic could not say the final notes brought him back to reality. They brought him back from reality. He didn't know if his eyes had been opened or shut; he felt as though he were hardly breathing. He joined in polite applause, but he felt as if others had had a glimpse of the Holy as he had. The service closed with murmured prayers and a brief litany of hallelujahs.

"Are you comin', Uncle Vic?" Davey's voice was as insistent as the gentle tug on Vic's shirt sleeve. Vic tousled his hair and stood to follow him. Milly and Dave were talking to another couple and Amy stood quietly between them and her brother.

"It was something, wasn't it, Uncle Vic?" she asked him. "I didn't know Lucy could sing like that. I would like to be able to sing like that. It makes you just think of Jesus, doesn't it?"

"Yes, Amy. Yes, it does."

Milly pulled him into their circle and introduced Vic to their friends. Vic looked around for Lucy, but didn't see her anywhere. He excused himself and went to look for her, but didn't find her in the small building. The pastor informed him that she had left right after the service. Vic returned to Dave and Milly and exited the front door with them.

"Does she always just disappear after her concerts?" he asked Milly.

"I don't know, Vic. It was absolutely. . .well, for once I'm at a loss for words. Anyway, we've never heard her sing before either, so I don't know if she always sings and runs. I'll have to call her and tell her how much we enjoyed it. Glad you came?" she asked brightly.

"Yes, I am. Thanks for the invite." He climbed into the van next to Dave and they drove home.

After the Fentons left Vic at his house, he pulled on his baseball cap and took Ralph for a walk. The service—no, the music had left him feeling melancholy and reflective. He walked the perimeter of the frozen lake at Keystone Park. Ralph kept a good pace when he wasn't sniffing around a bush and he was better behaved than usual when they passed other people and their dogs. They had just completed their full lap around the lake when Vic saw a woman sitting on a bench looking out over the lake. He wouldn't have noticed except that it was a really cold, breezy night again and the woman's head was uncovered. She wasn't wearing running shoes or boots like everyone else he had passed. It was Lucy.

"Lucy, are you all right?" he asked as he and Ralph came

closer to where she was seated. She startled, but smiled when she recognized Vic.

"Hello, Vic." She sat up straighter and held out a gloveless hand towards Ralph. "This must be. . .I forgot what you said his name was?" Ralph nuzzled her hand and then licked it.

"Ralph. Ralph, meet Lucy." Vic sat down next to Lucy while she petted Ralph's head. She seemed to momentarily forget Vic was there. He cleared his throat.

"I was at your church tonight with Dave and Milly and the kids. Your concert was wonderful, Lucy."

She rubbed Ralph's ears and stood up. "Thank you, Vic. G'night," she said, and promptly walked away.

Vic turned to Ralph who watched his new friend retreat into the dark towards the parking lot. "I think we've just been snubbed, old boy. Let's head home." The two returned home for the night, but it was a long time before Vic fell asleep.

The next day after his classes Vic called Milly to get Lucy's telephone number at work. Milly heartily squealed her approval. Vic had to cut her off quickly so she wouldn't have him promising to check out airfare prices or honeymoon packages. He quickly dialed Lucy's number before he changed his mind.

"Telephone Communications Service. This is Lucy. May I help you?"

"Lucy, this is Vic McCloskey. Did I catch you at a bad time?"

"Why, no, Vic. What can I do for you?"

Here goes, he thought to himself. "I wondered if you'd like to go to the basketball game Friday night—maybe go get a pizza first?"

"Well, I thank you for your offer, Vic." *Here comes the big rejection,* he thought. "I haven't been to a basketball game in years. It would be fun. What time?"

"Would six be too early?"

"Not at all. Got a paper and pencil? I'll give you my address and directions. Hold on a second, would you? I've got another call. . . ."

So it was on Friday that Vic McCloskey found himself sitting across from Lucy Evers at the pizzeria. In spite of the black mascara and the drawn-on eyebrows, Vic thought Lucy looked nice. Her royal blue sweater made her pale green eyes all the more intriguing. She had tried to cover her freckles with makeup, but they were persistent and he decided he liked them. They made her face interesting. Her boots made her almost as tall as he, which unnerved him a little. He had never dated such a tall woman before. He had shaved again in the afternoon, gotten a haircut the day before, and was careful to wear a lightweight sport shirt. He wanted to wear short sleeves, but thought she might bolt at the sight of his "hairier than a grizzly" arms. After they ordered their pizza, he thought it best to clear the air of any misconceptions immediately.

"I'm afraid I made a bad first impression on you, Lucy.

I didn't know you were going to be at the Fentons' that night for supper and felt a little uncomfortable and unprepared. I apologize if I offended you."

"Well, I wasn't at my best that night. And when I saw that you were the man I almost killed at the ski place, I was so mortified! I felt you must be thinkin' what a klutz I was. And I am. I'm always runnin' into things, into people, trippin' over my own two big feet. My whole life has been one near disaster after another. And here Milly had told you I could ski when I was just learnin'." She shook her head and Vic smiled at her embarrassment.

"You didn't 'almost kill' me, Lucy. I've had a lot worse falls all on my own." He nodded politely at one of his students who waved at him from across the room. It dawned on him why he usually didn't go out for pizza. Oh well, it would give his class of freshmen something to talk about.

"And to be honest, I was embarrassed to learn you are a Ph.D. when I just barely got through high school and work part-time cleanin' your office."

"Let's forget all that. Letters don't make a man or a woman. I want to talk about the concert the other night." She regarded him over her glass of cola and set it down. "It was. . ." he started, "it was like nothing I've ever been to before, Lucy. Your music. . .I don't know how to say this without sounding like some kind of mystic, but. . ."

"But it was like the music was singing itself? Like you were all alone with God?" He thought she was going to cry, but she didn't.

"Yes. It was like that. I can't even put into words what it

was like. It was wonderful and terrible all at the same time."
She shook her head in agreement and he had to lean across
the table to hear her.

"That's how it was for me, too. That has never happened
to me before. I could almost see Jesus Himself. It seemed the
music came from somewhere else—so deep inside me that I
didn't know a body could contain such beauty and delight
and still live. . . ." Their eyes held one another's and Lucy
smiled. "Nothin'. . .I mean, nothin' like that has ever happened to me before. That was why I left right away. . .and why
I didn't talk to you at the park. I couldn't. I just couldn't."
She hesitated. "It was like you said: wonderful and terrible
all at once. I'm glad you were there and sensed it too. It obviously can't be described. And at the time, I just couldn't
talk to anyone."

The waitress brought their pizza and their discussion
ended. Vic returned the greeting of another student and
smiled apologetically at Lucy.

"I had forgotten why I never eat out. I feel like a celebrity or a bug under a microscope."

"You never go out to eat?" Lucy asked between bites.

"Not with a woman, generally—at least, not in town.
I'd introduce you, but that's what we would end up doing the
rest of the night. A nod of my head and a look that says, 'stay
away from me or I'll flunk you' usually keeps even the most
curious at bay."

"Is it really that bad?" Her look was skeptical.

"Probably not, but this is a small college town and small
college towns lend themselves readily to gossip. In my last

position I was one person in a big university in a big city. Nobody noticed anyone there; the anonymity had its advantages for single men. There's always well-meaning friends trying to pair me off here."

"Friends like Milly Fenton?" Lucy asked with a knowing smile.

"Friends like Milly Fenton. You've been there, too," he said, reaching for another piece of pizza.

"She means well. And," Lucy finished the last of her cola, "here I am, sittin' across from Keaton's most eligible bachelor."

"Is that what Milly said?" He returned Lucy's teasing smile with a roll of his eyes.

"That is what Miss Milly said."

The rest of their conversation was light, friendly, and comfortable. Vic found himself laughing at stories Lucy told of her relocation to Keaton and how she had come to develop a friendship with Milly. It seemed to Vic that little time had passed when Lucy looked at her watch. She reached for her purse and pulled out her lipstick.

"Should we be goin'? It's a little cold in here." She shivered as she pulled on her coat. Vic thought it was comfortable and was glad he had left his coat in the car. He looked at his watch too and took a final drink of his beverage.

"Yeah, we had better leave. Hopefully we won't have to sit in the nosebleed section of the gym if we get there early enough."

Vic found Lucy almost as entertaining as the game, which Keaton won in the final seconds. He would clap and whistle, but she stood up most of the game, cheering, yelling, and grumbling (loudly) about some of the calls that were made. She clenched Vic's arm so tightly in the final seconds he thought his hand would fall off from lack of blood. She had managed to spill her soft drink on him at halftime, step on his bunion twice in her zealous cheering, and had almost tumbled onto the couple in front of them more than once. They scarcely talked, but Lucy was very vocal.

They remained in the stands after the game while the crowd thinned. Lucy collapsed back against the bleacher behind her and put her hand to her chest, breathing hard. She looked at Vic with eyes sparkling, her mascara slightly smudged, and her face pink. He thought her freckles looked darker. She giggled and brought the other hand up to rest on the recently scarred one.

"My, but that was some fun," she said, slowly drawing out the last two words.

"It was. I'm glad you came with me." Vic tried to wipe his damp forehead inconspicuously, but decided that was impossible and pulled out his handkerchief and wiped the perspiration from his brow. "What next? It's early yet. Would you like to get a cup of coffee or something?"

"Why not my apartment? It's not fancy, but it's quiet and you don't have to worry about any of your students showin' up."

"Sure. Let's go."

They drove to Lucy's in Vic's pickup truck with Vic telling Lucy about the town of Keaton itself and some of the local history. In answer to her questions, he told her about himself and his family, how he had come to be teaching at the local college, and a little about his classes and students. When they reached her apartment complex again, he felt like he had done most of the talking. She took his coat once they were inside and he sat down and took a slower look around than he had when he had picked her up.

The room was scarcely furnished and the furniture looked worn and old. Unlike his own living room, there were no pictures on the walls and the window coverings looked like they might have been left by previous renters. They were a drab green and Lucy's furnishings were navy and rust in color. He picked up the one picture that sat in the room. It was an older photograph of Lucy; she was thinner and had long hair, pulled back in a ponytail. She stood looking up at a little girl who sat on the back of a horse. *She looks like she has Down syndrome,* Vic thought. He would have guessed her to be about eight or so. Her hair was blond and she didn't look happy about sitting on the horse.

"Who's in this picture with you, Lucy?" he called to her. She came around the corner with two cups of coffee and sat down next to Vic.

"My daughter," she answered, handing Vic his cup and setting hers next to the picture. "Precious little thing, isn't she?" She picked up the photograph and looked at it lovingly. "Missy grew to love that horse, though you'd never know it by this picture." She set it back down.

"Your daughter? I didn't know you had a child. Milly's never mentioned it. Where is she?" This new information left

Vic somewhat uncomfortable.

"No, I don't suppose she did since I haven't mentioned it to her myself." Lucy took a drink of her coffee and regarded Vic intently for a few moments, as if weighing telling him more. "You've told me a lot about yourself, Vic. I suppose you should know somethin' of me. But first. . ." She surprised Vic by leaning towards him, touching her hand to his cheek and kissing him gently on the mouth. "Thank you for such an enjoyable evenin' after hearin' me talk of you so unkindly at that restaurant." His eyes widened. "After my friend and I left there that night, I saw you in the booth behind where we were sittin' and figured you'd heard ev'ry word I said. I apologize again; it seems I'm always apologizin' to you," she said with a shake of her head.

"Well, let me apologize too while we're at it." He lightly pressed his lips to hers and decided he liked it as well the second time as the first. He was glad she returned his kiss. "I'm sorry I made such a bad first impression. Now, tell me about you and Missy." He settled back against the couch and held his mug of coffee in both hands.

"I was a wild young thing as a kid—grew up in the hills, you know, and have a mess of brothers and sisters. I got pregnant when I was sixteen and had Missy. She had Down syndrome." She said her last sentence like a question, a voice inflection Vic was getting used to hearing her use. "But she was not badly affected. She learned quick and was a delight to her grandpappy and me. My momma didn't talk much to me after I got pregnant." Lucy paused before continuing.

"Anyway," she said, "I did finish high school, but my

heart wasn't in it. Missy's daddy, he was a big ole football star and had a scholarship and didn't want nothin' to do with a 'retard,' as he called her." Vic saw the set of Lucy's jaw and the way she lifted her chin.

She suddenly faced him again and smiled. "But her daddy repented of that sin when he was a little older and wiser—and I repented of my sexual sin and my hate for Missy's daddy when I got saved. But that's all past." She stopped before continuing. "When I was in my early twenties I had the accident. Missy and I were goin' to a concert I was gonna do when we collided with a truck. Missy was very badly injured and I was hospitalized myself and on life support for a few weeks. I recovered, but Missy was permanently brain-damaged and had to be put in an institution. She died a few years back, but I'm still payin' for all those years she spent in that long-term care facility. I put flowers on her grave ev'ry year on her birthday. It'll be a longer drive this year, but I decided some time ago I needed to get away from the ole hometown and venture out on my own.

"So, here I am in Keaton." She fingered the photograph lovingly and looked at it again on the table. "My daddy, he died soon after Missy, and Momma speaks to me now, but my brothers and sisters are spread out all over the country, so we don't see each other much. So," she said, turning her attention back to him with a rueful smile, "that's who is in the picture with ole Lucy and that's how I got to Keaton."

"I'm sorry about Missy, Lucy. I've yet to lose anyone in my family and we've never had any falling-out in the ranks or tragedy like you've known."

"Well, that's all past now. I really have had a good life and I treasure every year I had with Missy, even those years she didn't seem to know me or anyone else. She was still my little girl; she was still the one God gave me. Lovin' her taught me a lot about lovin' God. . .and even more about God lovin' us. Melissa Joy. She was a joy. . . ." She stood and held out her hand to Vic.

"Would you like another cup, Vic? Should I turn on the TV?"

"No, thanks, Lucy. Could I talk you into singing a song or two?"

She gave him a quizzical look as she returned the coffee cups to the kitchen. "Are you serious?" she asked.

"Yes. After that game I need something to soothe the spirit and the mind. How about it?"

"I have never, I mean never, had a date ask me to sing for him," she said as she went to her bedroom, returning with her guitar in hand.

"Have you dated a lot?" he asked.

"I've had my share," she answered somewhat coyly as she strummed the strings. "Now, that is bad." She quickly tuned the instrument and strummed several more chords. "What's your pleasure, sir?" she asked with a smile as she sat down.

"Something homegrown; something you've written."

"How do you know I have written anything?" she challenged.

"Because everyone south of the Mason-Dixon line is a born songwriter. Everyone born north of the Mason-Dixon line knows it," he retorted.

"Is that so?"

"That's so."

Lucy scratched her head briefly and began playing a tune he did not recognize. She gave him a conciliatory smile and he held up his hands in a gesture that said, "I'm waiting."

Lucy's gentle strumming and a few hummed notes made Vic smile in relaxed appreciation. He watched her fingers on the strings and her deep contralto voice mesmerized him. He closed his eyes and let the music and words draw him to her.

Come walk with me in the valley
  Come hold my hand in the sun;
As night closes in, again we'll begin
  To tender the blossom of love.
Come run with me in the meadow
  Come laugh at winds swirlin' 'round;
As clouds gather close and rain splashes down
  We'll tender the blossom of love.
Come climb snow-covered mountains
  Come know their bold majesty;
As cold embraces and strokes our faces
  We'll tender the blossom of love.
Come dance with me in the garden
  Come hold me close to your breast;
Tell me your dreams; tell me your heart
  Let's tender the blossom of love.
Come tell me your dreams,
  Come tell me your heart,
Let's tender the blossom of love.

She closed the song with a few more chords and smiled shyly at Vic.

"That was beautiful, Lucy. Thank you."

Lucy set the guitar behind the sofa. "It won't win any country music awards, but I wrote it for Missy. I sang it to her day after day. I would tell her of Jesus, sing some of the great hymns to her, and leave her each day singin' that song." She tucked her feet up under her. "You would have liked Missy, Vic," she continued. "She was a sweet child—sensitive, tender, innocent. And such a capacity for love! I do miss her. That's one reason why I left home; I needed to build my life without her. It was too painful livin' there any longer with her gone." She stretched her long arms and fingers out in front of her and brightened. "But that's all behind me now. I haven't sung that song for a long time. So, now you know all there is to know about me. Can I get you anything else, Vic? I've got some cookies. . . ."

Vic stood. "No. I'd better be going." He picked up his coat and put it on. "Thanks for the nice evening, Lucy."

"Thank you, Vic. Be careful goin' home."

Vic left without kissing Lucy good night. He was contemplative and somewhat melancholy. He admitted to himself that he had never yet come away from any time with Lucy feeling the same way. She was something of an enigma to him: wild swings in mood, each one as intense as the last, no matter how far removed. She was so unlike him. He changed little no matter what he was feeling. He would get angry, but never angry enough to become physical. He would get excited, but never excited enough to get very vocal. He would be serious—or happy—but one was never far from the other. He guessed he could be called content, possibly boring, depending on the disposition of anyone who might try to analyze him.

He weighed what he had so far concluded he and Lucy had in common. They were born-again believers, but they chose very different churches in which to worship. They both were music-lovers and both could sing, but he remembered Lucy saying over at Fentons' that she couldn't tolerate that "stuffy, longhaired classical junk" that did little more than put her to sleep. Vic thrived on the likes of Beethoven, Mozart, and all the great masters. He was always warm; she was always cold. He was highly educated, she was not. He shook his head. What did something like that matter? But he loved to read; he read voraciously. Lucy had told him that she never read anything but the Bible and the newspaper and often not even the newspaper. Vic liked women who didn't wear much makeup and preferred women who were petite. Lucy most assuredly overdid the cosmetics; her makeup was heavy, her cologne too strong, and he detested the acrylic nails she wore. She was not petite, she was clumsy, and she was outspoken. When he had dated other women of his choice, they were like him: reserved, generally quiet, and not demonstrative. Like him. The only time Vic had ever seen Lucy that way was the first time he had officially met her. She was probably out of character that night—ill at ease and weighing him as he had her. He gave Ralph a pat on the head as he walked into the house. Well, they had cleared the air of bad first impressions and had a pleasant date. He probably wouldn't ask her out again, however. They had little in common.

Vic wasn't quite sure how it came about a few weeks later that he, Lucy, Milly, Dave and their children found themselves at Milly's parents' winter cabin for a weekend. They trekked well over fifty miles in the snowmobiles on Saturday and came back to the cabin hungry. After their dinner, Dave went out with Amy and young Dave for another brief trip on their sleds. Vic washed the dishes and then sat down with a book he had been reading. Milly and Lucy were in the hot tub.

Lucy came into the high-ceilinged great room with her hair still damp at the ends and her face flushed. She had put on some jeans and a turtleneck sweater. She wasn't wearing any makeup and her pale green eyes were in marked contrast to the pink of cheeks and the deep coloring of her freckles. Vic took off his reading glasses and set his book aside. Lucy sat in front of the fireplace, her back absorbing its warmth.

"Where's Milly?" Vic asked.

Lucy fingered the wet ringlets at her neck and tilted her head forward to let the fire's heat dry her hair. "Takin' a nap. I suspect she might be pregnant. She thinks so and I think she's right. She hasn't said anything to Dave or the kids yet, so don't you," she warned, her voice muffled against her chest.

"No kidding! I didn't think they planned to have more children!"

"I don't think they did either, but the Lord had somethin' else in mind, I'd say." She looked up at him. "What are you readin'?"

"It's a book written by a young preacher in Nazi Germany who was martyred for his Christian faith in 1945."

"Is it a good book?" she asked, looking up at Vic.

"It's a little heavy, but good. Thought-provoking." He studied the color of Lucy's eyes. "You look nice, Lucy," he said simply.

"With no makeup and these ragged, guitar-pickin' fingernails?" She laughed. "I look like your cleanin' lady from work!" She stood and fanned her face. "Whew! After that hot tub even I'm too warm to sit by this fire. Want somethin' to drink?" She walked to the kitchen.

"No, I'm fine, thanks." He watched Lucy as she poured herself some coffee and came back into the room to stand before the large bay window that looked onto the dense woods behind them.

"This is a beautiful place, isn't it, Vic? You come here a lot with Dave and Milly?" She sat her coffee cup on the seat under the window and peered out the corner of the window. "Come look at this," she said.

Vic walked over to where she stood and looked to where she was pointing. A rabbit was placidly regarding them from his position near a large pine tree. He sat on his haunches, his nose wriggling and his breath visible in the cold air. The rabbit seemed to know he was safe. He turned his attention from them and hopped closer to the cabin, no longer watching them.

"There's lots of game around here. I thought you might be calling me over to look at a deer or two. Milly's dad keeps a salt block just beyond that tallest pine. I've been up here a few times with them and the kids, in answer to your question. Dave and I came up here last fall for a weekend with the three guys I'm discipling. It was a good time: studying, praying, fishing, just getting away. . ."

"I used to go to a place back in the hills where my daddy grew up. I went there a lot durin' Missy's years at Willow Springs. I wouldn't wear shoes the whole time I was there— just sit around thinkin' up music and songs and writin' them out. We're not so different, are we, Vic?" she asked, turning to face him. He chuckled and rubbed the back of his neck.

"It's funny you should say that. I was just thinking not long ago how different we are." Vic regarded her quietly and then gently pulled Lucy into his embrace and kissed her long and tenderly on the lips. He felt her arms wrap around his shoulders as she returned his kiss. He wasn't sure why he did it. He hadn't seen her much since their one date, and he certainly hadn't kissed her again since the brief kisses they had shared at her apartment.

She started to speak against his lips, but he drew her tighter to him.

"I think we are not so diff—" she repeated, but he silenced her with another kiss. Lucy stepped away from Vic after their second kiss, picked up her cup of coffee, and walked back to the sofa. Vic sat beside her and pulled an afghan over her.

"How did you know I was gettin' cold?" She pulled it up over her shoulders and snuggled against Vic.

"If I've learned anything about you in the last few months, Lucy, it's that you're always cold."

"And you're always warm," she returned.

"You noticed."

"I did."

"Like I said, I don't think we're much alike."

Lucy tucked her legs up under her on the couch and turned so that she was facing Vic. She laid her head against Vic's shoulder and he wrapped his arms around her. She raised her head and he was again struck with the uncanny color of her pale eyes.

"I'd say we're alike in some important ways—and different in some important ways too. . . ."

He kissed Lucy again and she returned his kiss.

"You know," he said against Lucy's hair, "Milly would like nothing better than to find us necking on the couch." Lucy giggled and shook her head.

"Now, ain't that the truth?" She slipped out of his embrace and laid her head on a pillow she placed at the opposite end of the sofa. "Why don't you just go back to your book and I'll lie here and watch your beard grow."

"So you noticed that too. I did shave this morning," he said with mock offense.

"Honey," she drawled, "You could shave mornin', noon, and night and it wouldn't make a bit of difference. But I've decided I like that about you. Why don't you read some of your book to me?"

"Good idea," he said.

He hadn't read three paragraphs and Lucy was asleep. "So much for a lot in common," he said quietly. He went back to reading his book silently.

He had been reading for about a half an hour when Dave and his children came back in. Their stomping feet and noisy laughter woke Lucy up. She looked at Vic sheepishly.

"Did I miss a good part?" she smiled, rubbing her eyes. She sat up and lifted the ends of her hair off the back of her neck. "Nothin' worse than layin' down on a wet head," she mumbled.

"Yes, you did. But that's okay; I'll lend you the book when I'm finished," Vic said, setting it down.

"Hey! Where's the woman of the house? We need some hot chocolate!"

"She's takin' a nap, David. I know how to heat water in the microwave; I'll get it. You kids want some too?" Lucy walked to the kitchen.

"Yeah!" Amy and Dave both answered at once.

"You should have come out with us, Uncle Vic. It was great!" Young Dave plopped down on the couch next to Vic.

"Amy," Dave called from the kitchen, "why don't you get a game out and go get your mom up? We can play something before we go out again." Amy did as instructed and went to get her mother.

"It's dark out now. What are we going to do outside next?" Vic asked as Dave came back into the room with two steaming cups of hot chocolate.

"We thought we would just take a short walk. We won't be able to stay late tomorrow, so we'll take a quick hike tonight, hit the sleds again tomorrow after we have our own little Sunday service, eat a quick bite and head back to Keaton. Davey's got something with the youth group going on and I need to be at church for a board meeting." He set the cups down on the table and Lucy followed with the other two.

"You be wantin' some, Vic?" she asked, turning back to

the kitchen. He shook his head "no" and moved to the table.

"Ah, here comes Sleeping Beauty now," Dave said.

Milly and Amy sat down across from Vic, and Lucy came back into the living room with a cup of the hot brew for Milly. She set it in front of her.

"This will wake you up, Mil. And I gave it an extra shot of whippin' cream." Lucy sat next to Vic and looked down at the game board. "You are not goin' to make me play Monopoly, are you?" she groaned.

"Just one game, Lucy," said the rosy cheeked Amy.

" 'One game' will last until the cows come home and then some," Lucy protested. Amy won out, however, and the game began. It did last long into the evening. Everyone went to bed without taking Dave's proposed hike.

After their morning "service" of singing, Davey and Amy praying aloud, and Vic reading from John 17, the entire group doubled up on the snowmobiles and went for a brief ride in the snow, blindingly white and silver beneath the unclouded sun. By the time they had packed up and driven the two-plus hours home, Dave was running late for his meeting.

"Just drop me at my place, Dave, and I'll run Lucy home," Vic volunteered.

"That would help out, Vic." He pulled their van into the drive and quickly helped Lucy and Vic unload their bags. With a wave and a round of good-byes, the Fentons were gone and Vic went around to the back to let Ralph into the house. Lucy opened the back door for them.

"Your house is beautiful, Vic," she commented as he came in, stomping snow from his boots. Lucy had walked over to peer into his study and nodded her head, smiling at him. "It's you, that's for certain. Very masculine and high-brow. I don't believe I've ever seen so many books—except maybe at the library. Have you really read all of these?" she asked, her eyes scanning the titles on his bookshelves.

"Most of them," he grunted, pulling his boots off. He threw his jacket over a kitchen chair and got a glass of water. "Anything to drink, Lucy?" he asked.

"No, thank you." She ran her hand along the dark mahogany of his desk. She sighed. "You have such nice things, Vic. I envy you a mite," she said, looking wistfully about the room.

"Well, I never had a daughter or relative in an extended-care facility. Things like that make short work of a paycheck." He signaled Ralph to come to him, away from Lucy.

"Could I see the rest of the house? Would you mind?" she asked.

"Of course not. There's not much to see, really," he said. He took her around the house, which didn't take long. He turned on the radio and showed her how he had wired the entire house for his sound system. The music of Brahms' first symphony followed them from room to room. They completed their circuit and ended standing in the living room.

"This really is lovely, Vic. With all your nice things and your classical music and your books and. . .Ralph." She smiled a small smile. "I have to agree with you. We're not much alike, are we?" She didn't give him a chance to answer. "Ready to take me home?" she asked brightly.

Vic found these quick changes in her mood and de-meanor exasperating. Lucy was contemplative and serious one second and light and nonchalant the next. He wasn't sure if he was amused or annoyed. He made a decision.

"Can we talk a minute first, Lucy?" he asked. He liked Lucy. He liked kissing Lucy. He liked listening to her sing. But he didn't want to lead her on or get involved with her—or any other woman—right now. So, he had better make it all clear today.

"Of course. About what?" she asked.

He motioned for her to sit down and he sat across from her and ran his hand back through his thick hair. He thought a few seconds before continuing.

"You know, don't you, that Milly is an incurable match-maker?"

"Do I know it? Why else is a poor little girl from Ten-nessee sittin' in the house of a well-to-do college professor?" she retorted, an understanding smile on her face. "I know you're doin' all this as a favor to Milly. She means well, but she's not the matchmaker she thinks she is."

"Now, that's not entirely correct. My invitation to you for the game a few weeks back was my idea." Vic felt as though the conversation had taken an unexpected turn. "What I'm trying to say is—"

"What you're tryin' to say, Vic, is that you don't want to get involved with anyone right now, but just want to be friends. Am I right?" Lucy stretched her long legs out in front of her and regarded Vic with a bemused look.

He wasn't going to be quite so blunt, but Lucy had said just what he was thinking. He had enjoyed kissing her, however, and wasn't sure he wouldn't enjoy it again. Well, he would sort all that out later. "Yes, Lucy, that's just what I wanted to say." *I think,* he said to himself.

"Good," she said, standing to her full height. "That's the way I feel too. But, who knows? It could change. But for now," she held out her right hand to him, "friends?" He stood too and clasped her hand in a single shake.

"Friends." He smiled at his friend and breathed a sigh of relief. "So," he continued, "as my friend, would you do me a big favor?"

Lucy picked up her purse and began pulling on her gloves. "Don't tell me; you want me to feed and walk Ralph while you go out of town for a few days." She again ended her sentence with a question in her voice.

Vic laughed as he picked up her bag and pulled his keys from his pocket. "No, it's worse than that. I have to attend a party at the home of one of my colleagues. If I go alone, I'll be at the mercy of his wife who has a 'very eligible, young, attractive,' etcetera daughter who will be there, I'm sure, for my benefit—"

"Another matchmaker?" She followed him to his truck and climbed in as he loaded Ralph into the back with a whistle and drop of the hatch. Ralph eagerly jumped in and Vic got in behind the steering wheel.

"You guessed it. Would you mind?" He started the truck and backed out.

"If you'll do the same for me," she replied. "I have a

Sunday school class function comin' up and this Walter fella just follows me around like a lost puppy at these things. He's a nice enough boy, but he is just a boy." She pulled her sunglasses back down over her eyes and pulled up the collar of her coat tighter around her neck.

"This already sounds like a friendship of convenience," Vic said.

"Friendships have been built on a lot less, I'd say," Lucy answered.

"I don't know about that," Vic replied. "But I think we really have more going than that. Don't you?"

"I do." She turned on the radio and listened to the weather forecast. "And do you accept my invitation to our class party in two weeks?" she asked.

"I do," Vic answered, turning the corner to drive to Lucy's.

So it was one year later that a new phase in their friendship began as Victor McCloskey and Lucy Evers repeated those same two words to each other at the altar of Lucy's small, storefront church. Milly Fenton heard them and gave her husband a satisfied, glowing smile over the head of her infant daughter.

"It won't be long and Lucy Victoria will have a playmate," she whispered.

"Probably not long at all," Dave concurred.

They were the first to applaud as the pastor introduced Dr. and Mrs. Victor McCloskey for the first time. As they waited their turn to greet Vic and Lucy in the receiving line, Milly nudged Dave with an elbow.

"Look, honey, there's Lucy's friend, Walter." She handed little Lucy to Dave.

"Yeah," he said disinterestedly, giving his newest daughter a kiss. "So what?"

"That friend of Lucy's from the telephone company is here. I think it's time someone introduced them. . . ." She left Dave standing alone with the baby. Dave walked to Davey and Amy, who were both in the wedding party.

Young Dave ran a finger under the collar of his rented tuxedo shirt. "Mom's at it again, isn't she?" he said to his father, shaking his head. He stroked the head of his baby sister fondly. "I will never," he said emphatically, "bring female friends home for her to meet."

His father put a hand on his growing son's shoulder. "That's right, son. You won't have to. She'll bring them home to you."